Hawai'i – Stolen Paradise

Hawai'i - Stolen Paradise
A Brief History

Stephanie C. Fox

QueenBeeBooks

Bloomfield, Connecticut, U.S.A.

Copyright April 2013 © by Stephanie Carole Fox

All rights reserved. Published in the United States by QueenBeeBooks, Connecticut.

Library of Congress Cataloging-in-Publication Data
Name: Fox, Stephanie C., author.
Title: Hawai'i – Stolen Paradise: A Brief History / Stephanie C. Fox.
Description: Connecticut: QueenBeeBooks, [2014].
Identifiers: ISBN: 978-0-9996395-8-0 (paperback)
Subjects: 1. United States – General—HISTORY. 2. United States – State & Local – General—HISTORY. 3. Oceania—History.

www.queenbeeedit.com

Cover design by Stephanie C. Fox
Cover photographs by Stephanie C. Fox
Printed in the United States of America

Also by Stephanie C. Fox

The Book of Thieves

The Bear Guarding the Beehive

*Elephant's Kitchen
– An Aspergirl's Study in Difference*

*Almost a Meal
– A True Tale of Horror*

An American Woman in Kuwait

*Scheherazade Cat:
The Story of a War Hero*

*Nae-Née
Birth Control: Infallible, with
Nanites and Convenience for All*

*Vaccine: The Cull
Nae-Née Wasn't Enough*

*New World Order Underwater
The Nae-Née Inventors Strike Back*

What the Small Gray Visitor Said

Intrigue On a Longship Cruise

*Hawai'i – Stolen Paradise:
A Travelogue*

This history is dedicated to
the people of Hawai'i
and to my parents.

I have my mother to thank
both for taking me to Hawai'i
and for editing this book.

Table of Contents

Writing a Brief History of Hawai'i 1
The Visits of Captain Cook 4
The Ancient Polynesians Arrive 7
The Hawaiian Culture 8
The Kamehameha Dynasty 10
Kamakahonu – The Kauhale of Kamehameha the Great 14
The Natural History of Pearl Harbor 16
Pu'uloa – Native Hawaiian Aquaculture 17
The Missionaries Arrive 20
Ka'ahumanu – The Literacy Queen 23
Kamehameha II 25
Kamehameha III 28
Princess Victoria Kamamalu 32
Kamehameha IV 34
Kamehameha V 37
Lunalilo Rules for Over a Year 41
A Hotly Contested Election 44
The Merrie Monarch 46
Princess Ka'iulani 50
A Reciprocity Treaty 58
Kalakaua Returns One Last Time 59
Queen Lili'uokalani 60
The Theft is Accomplished 65
The Queen Fights Back – With an Anti-Annexation Petition 67
Annexed Anyway 69
Not As the Big Five Planned It 71
A U.S. Naval Base 72
How the Big Five Ruined Hawai'i for Hawaiians 73
The Racist Haole Woman Who Lied 74

The Dishonor Killing 76
Battleship Row with the USS *Arizona* 78
World War II Deposes the Big Five 80
A Disparity of Resources 81
Tora! Tora! But No Third Tora 82
The Ni'ihau Incident 85
U.S. Concentration Camps 92
Cleanup and War 93
Peace and Creating a Memorial 96
Hawai'i Becomes Five-O in 1959 98
Bibliography 99
Glossary of Hawaiian Words 108
About the Author 112

Writing a Brief History of Hawai'i

This history was originally written as the prelude to a travelogue about a trip I took in October of 2012 to O'ahu and the Big Island. But…it was such a large project, both as an e-book and in print that I decided to release the history segment on its own for those who enjoy learning about the past of another culture.

Here is the history, as written for that travelogue, plus a significant portion of the history segment on Pearl Harbor. I hope you enjoy it as much as I enjoyed researching and writing it.

I don't write travelogues merely to revive pleasant memories.

I write them to share what I learn, and I love to learn things.

Not only that, but I care about the point of view that I take. In college, I minored in women's studies, so taking the position that Hawai'i was stolen from the Hawaiian people rather than belonging to a judgmental, invading, white malestreamed population comes naturally to me. Doing otherwise feels wrong and selfish.

The United States is a stolen nation. Granted, we aren't going to move. Things have gone on too long and too far for that. But we should acknowledge the truth in our histories.

As this history will explain, Hawai'i was stolen without the slightest excuse. The Puritans could at least claim religious persecution when they left for North America and landed at what came to be known as Plymouth, Massachusetts. Not so for the missionaries who came to Hawai'i to convert the people who lived there, and their sons who built economic empires for themselves.

The first thing I did when I began to study the Islands was to get an overview of them:

O'ahu – The Gathering Place: it has the capital city, lots of great beaches, and the royal family was based there when Hawai'i was still under their jurisdiction. That meant that O'ahu would have their residences and other historic sites of interest to me. I love history.

Writing a Brief History of Hawai'i

Mau'i – The Valley Isle: it is two sections, with a small northwest one connected by a valley to larger southeast one. What do people do on this one? They hike and enjoy the beach, for the most part.

Kaua'i – The Garden Isle: it is round, also mostly about nature and beaches, and many Hollywood movies were made there in the mid-twentieth century.

Moloka'i – The Friendly Isle: an ironic name, considering that the quarantine leper colony was on it, but there it is. Father Damian lived on that island, helping the lepers, until he foolishly stuck his finger in a common dish of poi and contracted the dreaded disease himself. It's another beach and hiking island.

Lana'i – The Pineapple Island: it has pineapple plantations, and 5-star golfing resort hotels.

Kaho'olawe – The Target Island: the U.S. Navy used it for target practice, made a terrible mess of it, and no one lives there.

Ni'ihau – The Forbidden Isle: a native population of Hawaiians live on it, it is privately owned by a family named Robinson, and visits are by invitation only, and only after a health inspection. The point of that is to ensure that the residents, whose immune systems are not primed against the Earth's pathogens due to their insulated existence, do not catch some lethal plaque from a visitor. The visitor could be immune to that pathogen, but a carrier. Also, the one Japanese pilot from the 2 waves that attacked Pearl Harbor to crash on the islands crashed on this one, and terrorized the residents for a couple of days until one of them killed him.

Hawai'i – The Big Island: the nation/state gets its name from this island…obviously…and it has active volcanoes on it.

Our trip took us to O'ahu and the Big Island of Hawai'i. Accordingly, I focused my attention of the historic sites of those islands. However, Ni'ihau proved to be too intriguing and of such historic significance that I wrote about its history as well.

Soon I was learning Hawaiian words, words beyond "aloha" and others that are familiar outside of the Islands. Most significant was "haole" – white foreigner. I began compiling a glossary, which appears at the end of this book, after the bibliography.

Hawai'i – Stolen Paradise

The material I found covered ancient history, oral Hawaiian history which was written down when the Hawaiian language acquired a writing system, the haole-missionary intrusion, the haole takeover of Hawaii, the haole apartheid culture that persisted after that, World War II, and statehood.

As I studied the history of the Islands, I could not miss Hawaiian language, culture, agriculture, aquaculture, music, dance, cuisine, or the Hawaiian people…nor would I wish too.

When we went on our trip, we found that everyone was welcoming, pleasant, and friendly, particularly the Hawaiians.

The Visits of Captain Cook

My research on Hawaiʻi began with the intriguing discovery that it was on the Big Island that Captain James Cook had died of what turned out to be stupidity. That was my assessment, concluded after a quick study of the tale.

Captain Cook had gone more than once to the Islands in the late eighteenth century.

He was mapping and exploring the islands of the Pacific, and had stopped in Mauʻi as he headed south. His benefactor was the Earl of Sandwich, so he named the place the Sandwich Islands, even though the people living there had already named it.

Eight weeks later, after visiting Samoa, Tahiti, and various other places, he came to the Big Island of Hawaiʻi. As he traveled, he kept giving all of these places new names in English, regardless of the fact that the people who were already living there had already chosen their own names for their own native islands.

Now he was back, but on another one of the Islands – the Big Island of Hawaiʻi. He arrived in Kealakekua Bay in late 1778. When his ship, the *H.M.S. Resolution*, was sighted by the residents, they thought that it carried the god Lono because its sails resembled Lono's standards. Lono was the god of fertility and agriculture, so he was important. As a result, when Captain Cook disembarked and went ashore, he was greeted as a god.

At first, his forays into the culture had gone well for him, and for his crew. He was treated like a god due his status as the leader of his group and to the fact that his skin tone differed from that of the native population. The women entertained (had sex with) his crewmembers. This intrigued the English; the native women were obviously not prostitutes, but their culture did not inhibit them from rowing out to the ship, boarding it with lei for the crew, and then spending the night. Added to all this was the fact that it was still the growing and hunting and fishing season during Cook's first visit.

But when he and his crew shoved off into the Pacific Ocean in early 1779, one of the masts of their ship broke, forcing them to turn back. When they arrived, it was during the four-month period of rest when the Hawaiians traditionally played games and lived off the supplies they had amassed during the rest of the year. And since it was a small island society, resources were finite.

Cook and his crew were greeted with a somewhat cooler reception this time.

A visiting foreign ship, regardless of whether or not it harbored a god, was full of people who would use up a large amount of resources. The annoyed Hawaiians decided that as long as Cook's crew was there to chop down a huge koa tree and make a new mast out of it, they might as well take a canoe ride, and shoved off in one from the *Resolution*.

Cook was worried – would he get it back? How would he and his crew manage without that canoe? That was when he made a colossally and lethally stupid decision: he grabbed a hostage, and chose the chief, Kalani'opu'u.

Well, what happens whenever one physically threatens the leader of any society?

That leader is typically surrounded by a group of individuals whose duty it is to handle his or her personal security. It's just not wise to bother that individual.

One of the security force, an ali'i – that's Hawai'i's chiefly caste, the one with warriors and governors – stabbed Cook.

He bled.

Wow….blood! That meant that he wasn't a god – he was just a different human, which made sense, since he wasn't from Hawai'i! They stabbed him some more, and he fell face down in the shallow waters off the coast of southwestern Hawai'i, at Kealakekua Bay. He drowned quickly.

Cook's men didn't just stand around gaping as this happened; four of them rushed to his aid and got killed, and two more were wounded.

The Hawaiians, once it was over, felt bad about the whole thing. Cook had been a pleasant enough guest on the previous visit, and this was clearly just a terrible misunderstanding. They took his body and gave it a decent funeral…according to their own culture, which was all that they knew. They reduced his corpse to its bones, and interred them high in the mountains.

Cook's remaining crew was allowed to finish fixing the mast (reasonable – how else did the Hawaiians expect them to be able to leave?), and then they found out about the funeral.

With difficulty, they managed to communicate that they had to bring what remained of Cook home to his wife, er, widow, Elizabeth, and could they please have it all back?

The Hawaiians wrapped it all up and gave it back.

What a mess.

Captain Cook had not been the first visitor from Europe to come to the Islands. A Spanish ship had been there two and a half centuries earlier, and at least two sailors had elected to stay permanently. There isn't much documentation about that, in part because Hawaiians kept track of their history through memory and oral recounting rather than writing it down.

At the time of Cook's "visit", there were roughly 300,000 Hawaiians living on the Islands.

The Ancient Polynesians Arrive

The first people to live on the Islands arrived, according to most recent estimates, around 300 C.E. They rowed themselves there from the southwest, originating from the area of Tahiti, Samoa, Aotearoa (that's what the Maori people call New Zealand), and other nearby islands. They did so in long pairs of connected canoes with a covered area in the middle, and with a large sail over that. The travelers knew astronomy to guide them.

They carved petroglyphs in rocks, and created songs that were unique to each individual so honored. The fact that oral rather than written history was the normal way of remembering the past was not a mark of anything other than the Hawaiian people's difference from the Europeans. They used what they had, not because they were primitive but because they had nothing else and because they understood that it was finite and so could not be wasted.

The travelers had brought pigs and chickens with them, and skills. They knew how to grow crops, how to fish, and how to make canoes, which they called *na wa'a*. (In Hawaiian, the word *na* is used to make a noun plural, while the noun is left as is. The word *wa'a* means canoe.)

The Hawaiians made clothing out of tree bark by pounding it into soft cloth with a *kapa*, making short loincloths for men called *na malo* and long sarongs for women called *na pa'u*. The aristocrats were advised by *na kahuna* of various kinds. There were priests, political advisors, and others. A kahuna is an expert of whatever field that the kahuna has studied in depth.

The Hawaiian Culture

For over a millennium, the Hawaiian people lived on the eight islands, developing their own dialect of the Polynesian language, which became their own branch of it after that much time in isolation. Their religious beliefs went on undisturbed and, not surprisingly, the volcano goddess Pele figured prominently in their thoughts.

There were wars, there was peace, and the chiefs became known as ali'i, which meant the ruling class. They tended to be very, very tall people who spent their childhoods developing their athletic skills and learning how to govern the common people with the advice of the kahunas around them. The high chief was called the ali'i nui.

The closer that a member of the ali'i could prove her or his lineage to the ancient gods and goddesses, the more mana, or spiritual power, she or he had. This was all oral history, so the people's memories were very strong, well-versed, and devoted to rote memorization for accuracy. Nothing was written down, and there was a lot to remember: history, lineage, lore, songs, skills, crafts, social mores, and so on and on.

The people spent their time fishing, growing crops, making canoes, building a one-room hale for each family out of koa wood and long strands of dried leaves, beating tree bark into cloth and dying it or drawing patterns on it. The ali'i, the chiefly caste of aristocrats, took part of what the people produced as taxes, and traveled around with the king and his household touring each island to check on the welfare of the people.

Both common people and rulers enjoyed a variety of entertainments in their spare time. These entertainments included games, sports, hula dance, singing, song creation (done from memory, not by writing), and chants.

For four months of each year, the people rested, living on their efforts of the other months. It was a kapu time, both sacred and taboo to interfere with. An ancient kapu system was in place during Kamehameha I's time, and he would not think of relaxing or abolishing it. One of the customs associated with it was that common people would drop close to the ground if the king or a member of the ali'i passed, so as not to let their shadow fall on that individual.

Hawai'i – Stolen Paradise

A good chief would visit the common people at their croplands and fishing villages without staying in their homes, camping nearby with the ali'i who traveled with him. A bad chief would stay in some random hale, turning out the farmer or fisher, and not reining in his ali'i companions, instead leaving them to sleep with the women of the family at night. A bad chief could get himself killed and replaced by operating that way.

Wars were fought from time to time over territory, until Kamehameha the Great finally united all eight of the Islands under his rule in the late eighteenth century. After that, there was peace among the Hawaiians, and just in time, as a new threat had discovered the existence of the tropical paradise: haoles, or foreigners.

The Kamehameha Dynasty

Kamehameha I became known as Kamehameha the Great. He had spent most of his reign in battle, fighting for control of island after island until he had united them under his rule. After that, peace ensued among the Hawaiian people, who had a friendly culture in such conditions.

Kamehameha was seven feet tall, and Ka'ahumanu was not his only wife. She herself was six feet seven inches tall. An ali'i is typically a towering, tall individual, someone who is charged with the people's safety and security. In a non-industrialized, natural society, the biggest, strongest, tallest individuals are the most imposing, intimidating, and capable of defending the people. No one would consider messing with or fail to respect someone like that.

Kamehameha the Great, as the first of five kings to bear that name, was responsible for uniting the eight islands, so he became Hawai'i's first reigning monarch in the late eighteenth century, when he was a young man. He lived to be sixtysomething…the exact year of his birth is not known.

He was born circa 1750, though other estimates have suggested 1735. Before he could conquer them all, a prophesy warned him, Kamehameha would have to build a massive temple – called a heiau – to his war god. He had this done in 1790. It worked. By 1795, he had conquered all of the Islands but Kaua'i. The chief of that island surrendered to him rather than have his people suffer a battle such as those on O'ahu had suffered, being pushed over the cliffs to their deaths. Ni'ihau, the westernmost islands, was part of that deal.

Conquering and uniting the islands had been a common goal among the warring ali'i chiefs, but Kamehameha I accomplished it in part because of the presence of European ships. Another reason was the stupidity of one of the ships' commanders: British captain Simon Metcalf visited Kona, invited a lesser ali'i aboard his ship, and then humiliated him – by yelling at him and having his bosun beat him – for some incomprehensible (to the guest) breach of the ship's rules.

Kamehameha swore revenge when he found out about it, and as luck would have it, the next ship to appear was commanded by Metcalf's son Thomas. It was the *Fair American*, and soon it was under new ownership. Payback was swift; the Hawaiian warriors boarded it as if to trade, then tossed the haoles overboard and beat them in the water until they drowned. One haole escaped, Isaac Davis. He was allowed to live, but had to adapt to life in a strange, new culture. When Simon came back, looking for his son's ship, a search party came ashore. One man, John Young, got separated from the group, and Kamehameha kept him.

Now Kamehameha had two haoles. They could not go home. The Hawaiian king was clever; he had no intention of killing either one of them, nor of making their lives miserable. He intended to learn all that he could about the haoles, since it was obvious that, likely sooner rather than later, so many more of them would arrive that an attack would not get rid of them. The king found both Young and Davis ali'i wives, and made them his advisors. They joined the kahunas of the court, and showed Kamehameha how to use the weapons aboard the captured ship.

Once he had united the Islands, Kamehameha did what became a tradition with the ali'i nui: he made a home base for himself, but left frequently to make the rounds of each island, visiting the people there, checking in with the ali'i who was governor of it, and then returning home. He had his own transportation for that, a royal wa'a (canoe).

In this painting by Herb Kane (in the lobby of the Courtyard Marriott King Kamehameha's Kona Beach Hotel), an aging Kamehameha is on the right, greeting a visitor, while his favorite wife, who later became what I like to think of as the Hawaiian literacy queen, Ka'ahumanu sits at the left.

Ka'ahumanu was a strong-willed and intelligent woman. She was also her husband's favorite wife. He had another whom he had married earlier, and who was queen alongside her but that other wife was chosen merely because her lineage was "purer" than Ka'ahumanu's. There were also other wives. But it was Ka'ahumanu who Kamehameha loved. He was very jealous and possessive of her, and he demanded that she not take any other husbands.

When I read that, I was fascinated. So Hawaiians had practiced not only polygamy, but polyandry also! Of course, that ceased when the Christians taught them about Calvinism, and insisted that their religion was better than that of the Hawaiians. Still, equal time...

The common people and the ali'i each wore similar clothing – a short malo wrapped around the waists of each kane (man) and a long pa'u wrapped around the waist of each wahine (woman) – but the ali'i had some additional accoutrements that set them apart.

An ali'i woman (or man) would wear a necklace called a lei niho palaoa made of braided human hair with a carved ivory or whale tooth dangling in front. A woman would also have a feather lei around her hair, and another one, called a lei hulu manu, around her neck. She also wore tortoise shell and/or bone bracelets. An ali'i man would wear a fitted mahiole (helmet) and cape or long cloak made of fine netting crafted from olona wood with human hair used to fasten feathers to the mesh.

The feathers came from birds with red and yellow plumage: the 'i'iwi bird was the source of the red feathers, which grow all over its body, so the Hawaiians would eat it. The yellow feathers came from the mamo and 'o'o birds. The 'o'o bird's feathers were mostly black, with yellow ones only near the wings and on its tail. The Hawaiians would catch them, pluck the feathers, and release them. Unfortunately, the 'o'o bird went extinct anyway...after the haoles arrived.

The yellow feathers showed higher rank than the red. The ali'i nui – high chief or king – could wear all yellow, while the governor chiefs had capes and helmets with lots of red feathers. The best way to explain the value of these feathers as work materials and the capes as completed products is to express it in terms of money.

In the mid-nineteenth century, the long, all-yellow, feather cloak that Kamehameha the Great wore was valued at approximately a million dollars. Just as haoles had their gold and gemstones, Hawaiians had their feathers. Each one was impressive, special, and of great value.

Hawai'i – Stolen Paradise

Beautiful feather kahili were made for each member of the royal family, in pairs. These were tall poles with cylindrical arrangements of feathers at the top. Ancient kahili included the bones of vanquished enemies. The kahili pair was carried by attendants throughout the life of the ali'i wherever she or he went, and when the ali'i sat down to eat or rest, they would be waved above, for fanning and cooling.

These are two kahili from the Kahili Room in the Bernice Pauahi Bishop Museum. They are original artifacts that belonged to members of her family.

Kamakahonu
– The Kauhale of Kamehameha the Great

A kauhale is a compound of household buildings for the ali'i nui, including a men's eating house, a women's eating house, a house to sleep in, a cooking shed, another shed for a canoe, and whatever else a family of aristocrats might want or need. A hale is just one building, and the ali'i nui is the high chief/king. When that living arrangement was standard for Hawaiian leaders, this was what Kamehameha the Great had.

He chose to make his home base on the Big Island of Hawai'i, at Kailua Beach in Kona, on the leeward side of the island. He was born at Kohala, north of Kona, but he chose this spot after conquering several islands and uniting the remaining ones under his rule via diplomacy. Like many other kauhale compounds, this one had a fishing pool for the chief's exclusive use, with shrimp in it. Kamehameha called his home Kamakahonu, and kept the kapu system in place, convinced that prophesies about his success in uniting the islands were connected to that system.

In the late 20th century, a group of Hawaiian historic preservationists decided to reconstruct and forever maintain a part of Kamakahonu. They did a beautiful job of it – at least, to a haole like myself, it looked amazing. They didn't recreate the entire kauhale; only one hale, with ki'i placed all around it. A ki'i is a tall, thin, wooden, carved image of a Hawaiian deity. In pre-haole times, groups of these images were placed all around the ali'i nui's kauhale and at any heiau. There is a native species of wood that grows on the Hawaiian Islands called koa, and this was used for the ki'i carvings.

After the missionaries established themselves and their beliefs on the Islands, they demanded that each heiau be broken down, and all ki'i images destroyed. Fortunately for history, posterity, archaeology, and the preservation of the Hawaiian cultural identity, some Hawaiian people did not comply with this demand. Instead, they hid many ki'i images. When Kamakahonu was being recreated, many of them were brought out and placed around it.

Clearly, the Hawaiians were adept at hiding things so well that they could not be found.

Hawaiʻi – Stolen Paradise

When Kamehameha the Great died, long wooden spears were crossed in front of his doorway. His son left until the kapu was lifted by the kahuna priests.

Kapu means taboo. A taboo is put on anything that is deemed sacred, but that is not all that there is to it. Sometimes a thing is simply considered a bad act, and thus is deemed kapu. Under the kapu system, Hawaiian women did not have any control of the common food supply. They were forbidden to eat fish, pork, coconut, or bananas. They also had to eat separately from men.

A typical funeral for an aliʻi lasted for weeks, and the songs that had been composed at his or her birth would be sung. The kahili set would be held or placed around the body. The common people would wail, keen, and mourn with tremendous energy. Some would even smash out their own front teeth in their grief. This practice was discouraged by the missionaries.

To this day, no one – well, no haole – knows where Kamehameha the Great was buried.

I did say that the Hawaiian people were adept at hiding things.

Kamakahonu, the recreation of the home of Kamehameha the Great. The view looks south along the coast of Kailua Kona. No haoles – or non-preservationists, for that matter – may enter. A sign out to the right across that walkway says "Kapu – Keep Out."

The Natural History of Pearl Harbor

With eight islands, Hawaiian rulers moved around a lot. They had to personally visit each one, to see and be seen by all of their subjects, and make sure that things were run smoothly by each island governor.

There are three large bays – or lagoons – on the southern side of Oʻahu that are actually a submerged river delta. When the sea level rose, the result was that a harbor with three sections, now called lochs, was formed: the West, Middle, and East Lochs. It was a maximum of forty deep in some places in its natural state, and shallower in other areas. The East Loch is the part that is known as Pearl Harbor, and it is the largest one. It has a large island in it, which is now called Ford Island.

Streams from the two volcanic mountain chains on Oʻahu, the Waiʻanae and the Koʻolau Mountains, still feed the former river delta. The tide from the Pacific Ocean keeps the water of Pearl Harbor and the other lochs fresh, just as it has for millennia.

The island of Oʻahu formed by a combination of tectonic and volcanic activity. The tectonic plate that the Hawaiian Islands sit on moved northwest, and the volcanic plume that formed them, which is still forming more islands today, produced Oʻahu by making those two mountain chains. Extinct volcanic craters – the Punch Bowl, Diamond Head, and Koko – sit east of Pearl Harbor.

Once formed, the land sat as fresh volcanic soil, ready for life to grow on it. Life blew to the Islands, bringing seeds, and birds flew over the islands, dropping more microbes in their excrement. Gradually, Oʻahu became covered with vegetation of many kinds, and various species of birds took up residence on it and the other Islands.

Pearl Harbor benefited from this process, and a wetlands formed on its shores. Birds nested there, and fish and shellfish spawned and grew in it. Oysters still grow in Pearl Harbor. Coral grew on top of the lava rock in its waters, and limestone formed the shore.

Pu'uloa – Native Hawaiian Aquaculture

The Hawaiians lived on the Islands – alone – for at least a millennium. They named the lagoons first, and they chose to called this place Pu'uloa, which means Pearl Harbor. They arrived in long, double-canoes with outrigger sails and a small covered structure for shelter from the elements, called wa'a. They could fish as they sailed, so the Polynesians, as they were called until they settled the Islands, arrived skilled and ready to benefit from Pu'uloa.

Once they had arrived and settled on O'ahu, it was not in the harbor. The Hawaiians lived inland, and used Pu'uloa as a food source only, because the place was marsh, reefs, and wetlands, with tall grasses but no solid ground to build a hale on.

Pu'uloa made a great food source, with ducks, terns, and other birds to catch, and a huge menu of both saltwater and freshwater fish, and shellfish to enjoy. The Hawaiians hunted finfish with nets and spears in their canoes, but they also grew certain species of fish in specially fashioned enclosures in the harbor.

Hawaiian aquaculture was a sophisticated endeavor. Some very basic, no-frills hale were built for the people who maintained the human-made fishponds in the harbor, while everyone else lived farther inland. The fishponds themselves were built by choosing two points of land that could be most easily connected by making a rock wall with at least one gate in the middle.

The rock wall would be mostly underwater, with part of it showing above. The gate, or makaha, was made of wooden slats lashed together. This allowed water to circulate in and out with the tide, so that the water inside the fishpond stayed clean and full of nutrients, while wastewater from the fish living inside washed out. Fish could swim in, but once they grew larger, they were trapped inside.

The fishponds were called loko i'a. They were both inside Pu'uloa and on the coast next to it. The ones inside Pu'uloa were called loko 'umeiki. The freshwater fishponds were inland from the coast, fed by underground water that came from the mountains. They were called loko wai. Their sizes varied with the sizes of the areas that could be enclosed. Nature formed random shapes in random sizes, so the Hawaiian aquaculturists built accordingly.

Puʻuloa – Native Hawaiian Aquaculture

The fish in these ponds were raised for the aliʻi.

The oysters that grew in Puʻuloa were valued solely for the food inside, not the pearls. There were two varieties; one grew up to six inches across. For a long time, until Kamehameha the Great, the pearls were cast aside. The Hawaiians cared only for the oyster shells after enjoying the food in them. It was kapu – forbidden – to speak while harvesting oysters.

They made fishhooks out of the shells, and carved them into white eyes for kiʻi images, and for teeth to line the edges of wooden paddles. The shells were also useful as scraping tools. The beautiful, shimmering insides of the shells attracted the Hawaiians with artistic talents, including a great-granddaughter of Kamehameha the Great, Princess Bernice Pauahi Bishop. There is a whole oyster shell that she is thought to have painted a scene inside, on display in her museum.

The scene painted inside this oyster shell is likely of the house that Princess Bernice Pauahi lived in with her husband, Charles Reed Bishop, before his career as Hawaiʻi's first banker took off and they moved to a mansion.

Once foreigners arrived in the Hawaiian Islands, the people found out that the pearls inside oysters were valuable as well. There weren't very many pearls, and their shapes were irregular. Kamehameha the Great promptly put a kapu on pearls so that he could have a trade monopoly from the jewels. He needed a source of revenue; the foreigners all dealt in money, a thing that was a novelty to the Hawaiians. This played a role in depleting the oyster beds of Puʻuloa.

Foreigners – haole – were going to be a problem for the Hawaiians in many ways. They would have a huge impact on Puʻuloa. As the nineteenth century wore on, they made pastures for livestock that they imported and built sugar plantations on Oʻahu. Runoff from their crops polluted it with silt and mud. It deprived the waters of oxygen by filling up the harbor until it wasn't as deep as it had been in many places.

A marine biologist would explain that a healthy pond has at least three temperatures due to a sufficient depth to accommodate them. Having these temperatures is what enables algae and fish crops to grow and thrive season after season. Without that, the fish and oyster beds did not have the environment they needed to continue as abundantly as before.

Added to that was the fact that the haole traffic was affecting the fishponds and oyster beds in a dramatic way. The aquaculture system was being rapidly dismantled to accommodate first the mast ships that brought the missionaries and then the steamships that brought and carried away the goods that the haole newcomers bought and sold. Natural coral reefs were disturbed to accommodate this. Wharfs, quays, docks, and moorings were constructed as well.

By the late nineteenth century, Puʻuloa was being referred to as Pearl Harbor. Its natural appearance had been replaced in large part by a human-made, artificial one. It looked a lot more haole than Hawaiian, with haole demands for its future to match.

The Missionaries Arrive

Things changed when the missionaries from New England arrived in the early nineteenth century. They were Calvinists who believed that work brought one closer to heaven, and that sex, music, dance, and enjoyment were sins. This was the exact opposite of what the Hawaiians believed.

Nevertheless, the Hawaiians did not get angry and tell them to pack up and go.

Why not?

The best answer I can glean from all that reading is that the king, Kamehameha II, and his kuhina nui (regent), Queen Ka'ahumanu, realized that the Calvinists came from a technologically developed society, and that there were many, many more of them who would follow. It was clear to these ali'i that the only way they could hope to cope with that and thus protect their people would be to learn all about them and adapt to as many of their ways as they found feasible.

Having had the advantage of interacting with John Young and Isaac Davies, and thus learning about the technological capabilities of the haoles, Kamehameha II and Ka'ahumanu felt forced into accepting the Calvinists. They arrived shortly after Kamehameha I had died and Ka'ahumanu was installed as regent, but he had anticipated this. After all, that was why Kamehameha the Great had captured and assimilated John Young and Isaac Davis. This foresight proves that people from less technologically advanced civilizations are as intelligent as those who have developed technology.

A recurring theme was about to play out, as it had in the past. Whenever Europeans traveled, they would force religious and cultural conversions on whatever society they met, insisting that their ways were the best…until people around the planet began to speak up and tell them otherwise. That ethnocentric and xenophobic attitude persisted until much damage was done to many cultures, and because of it, Hawaiians have lost the practice of speaking their own language to such an extent that few of them now know how to do it.

It seems that the desirable "gifts" to the Hawaiians from foreigners have been few: written literacy, convenient cotton for clothing, and the right of women to eat any food they wish. Ka'ahumanu put a stop to the ancient kapu system as a widow when, along with Queen Keopuolani, she broke the eating kapu.

Keopuolani was even happier to do this than Ka'ahumanu was, because her manu was so high that she had been living in near isolation. This was because, under the kapu system, if a commoner so much as saw her, he or she would most likely be put to death. Kamehameha himself was always careful never to let his shadow fall on her. Keopuolani was happy to stop living under such terms. Also, after long and careful consideration, Ka'ahumanu chose to convert to Christianity.

The unwanted gifts to the Hawaiian people have been many and damaging: leprosy, syphilis, gonorrhea, loss of their language, their livelihoods, near-loss of their beloved hula dance, the introduction of many non-native species (including the mongoose and rats that have caused more problems than anything else), and finally, the loss of their nation's sovereignty.

This was accomplished by a slow and hostile takeover, first of their culture by the missionaries, and next by economics, perpetrated by both the missionaries' sons as they grew up to be big businessmen, as well as by some other haole arrivals. Finally, those same men, in their late middle age, along with their sons, dissatisfied by the concessions granted to them by the royal family, resorted to force.

The missionaries disapproved of hula dancing, and did their utmost to persuade the Hawaiians that it was shameful to dance, male or female, while wearing only grass skirts and shaking one's body to show it off. They disapproved of dancing and singing most evenings and on into the night rather than spending that time in quiet prayer and study. The list went on, and the missionaries devoted themselves to finding willing converts to their way of thinking.

That was not an easy task, self-appointed though it was.

Imagine how the Hawaiians must have felt as total strangers, men and women, showed up on their shores wearing many more layers of cloth than could be practical or comfortable in a tropical climate, then started crying and turning their heads away as they looked at the people who lived there! The Hawaiians must have sensed that resistance would ultimately be futile, yet felt insulted, invaded, and imposed upon. I would have.

The Missionaries Arrive

Among their converts was David Malo, a Hawaiian who learned to read and write in Hawaiian. He wrote a book entitled *Hawaiian Antiquities*. It describes Hawaiian life and culture as it was before the missionaries arrived, detailing fishing and farming practices, including sophisticated methods of aquaculture, the making of clothing out of tree bark, games and other amusements, and the interaction of the common people with the aliʻi.

Oddly, there was one Hawaiian custom that the missionaries did not devote huge amounts of energy to changing: hanai. Hanai is adoption. It could be done for orphans or non-orphans; there were more reasons for it than just to make sure that every child had a home with parents. A significant reason for hanai was to share children with childless couples who were upset about not having their own children. Another was to forge emotional alliances by sending one's children to live with another aliʻi couple. The purpose behind that was to prevent wars from ever starting. If the hanai children grew up with two sets of parents, they would grow up to love both, and to want peace with both.

Ka'ahumanu – The Literacy Queen

Queen Ka'ahumanu should be forever remembered as Hawai'i's Literacy Queen.

It was she who saw the virtual writing on the wall of her nation's history and realized that since most other nations had a written language, so must hers. Not only that, all Hawaiians must learn it. She set an example to her people by being among the first to do so, and ordered that everyone else follow suit.

This portrait of Queen Ka'ahumanu, the literacy queen, is on display in the lobby of the Courtyard Marriott King Kamehameha's Kona Beach Hotel.

The effect of this was that Hawaiians were ready for political participation in the future, regardless of the form that their government might take. No matter what happened, no one would be able to say that the Hawaiian people were not qualified to assume the duties of any subject, citizen, or whatever one might call a natural resident of their nation. The Hawaiian people have consistently taken an interest in their own political affairs, and she prepared them well to defend their ability to do so.

Ka'ahumanu – The Literacy Queen

She was the favorite wife of Kamehameha the Great. He demanded that she not take any other husbands than himself because she was so important to him. Ancient Hawaiians (not really so ancient – this is only 2 centuries ago!) practiced polyandry as well as polygamy.

Very few drawings of Queen Ka'ahumanu were made when she was alive. One shows her sitting at court, outside on the ground with her kahili in hand and another pair of kahili being waved over her head by attendants, with her hair down long. She is wearing a long pa'u made of soft, beaten kapa cloth. She is a very tall, large, imposing woman, and it shows even as she sits staring fixedly at a spot on the ground, lost in thought. Another is a regal portrait of her, and still another shows her sitting at Kamakahonu, enjoying another lovely day at her husband's court. These last two were done by artists in the late 20th and early 21st centuries.

Kamehameha II

Liholiho took over when his father died, having grown up in a time of peace, never having known military conflict. He was the eldest child of his father and Queen Keopuolani, with two younger siblings, a brother named Kauikeaouli and a sister, Nahi'ena'ena. His brother would rule after he did. The boy was only five years old when his older brother became the new king.

Nahi'ena'ena was the first wahine ali'i to have a feathered cloak made for her, and it is on display today in the Hawaiian artifacts room of the Bernice Pauahi Bishop Museum. She did not live a happy life; the missionaries put her at war with her cultural upbringing. Half grown up, she had been destined to marry Kauikeaouli, who was just a year older than she was.

This was considered a sacred right in pre-missionary haole culture, a normal way of preserving the ali'i status and mana of the children that the couple would have. The missionaries, however, shamed her terribly, telling her that the match would be a mortal sin. It is unfortunate that scientists were not there instead to teach her about the genetic damage that such unions can inflict upon offspring.

Nahi'ena'ena suffered emotionally because of the missionaries, married the governor of Mau'i, and died at a young age of a broken heart. It was 1836; she was either 20 or 21 years old. Her treatment by the missionaries was somewhat ironic as Liholiho already had at least two wives, and his favorite was Queen Kamamalu, his half-sister by one of his father's other wives, Kalakua.

Princess Nahi'ena'ena's pa'u of 'o'o yellow feathers. She was the only Hawaiian princess ever to have such a cloak made for her. It is on display in the Hawaiian Hall of the Bernice Pauahi Bishop Museum.

Kamehameha II

But during Nahi'ena'ena's eldest brother's 5-year reign, she was witness to a less stressful change: the demise of the kapu system. Ka'ahumanu wanted it gone, and had for a long time. With her husband dead, she took two other husbands and pressured Liholiho relentlessly to break kapu publicly by eating at the women's table.

At last, Liholiho did so, silently getting up from the men's table, sitting down at the women's table, and eating. The people watched in amazement, then paused to consider that nothing else happened. Life just continued. The kapu system was over. Their religious belief that the ancient gods would be disturbed had been successfully challenged, and the missionaries struck, stepping in to fill the void in Hawaiian society with their own religion.

Meanwhile, Liholiho had some other issues to deal with, particularly economic ones.

He had begun to dress as a European king, in a red military uniform with gold feather trim (Hawaiian colors, at least), and his wives dressed as European queens, in the fashions of the haoles. The haoles demanded the right to own land in Hawai'i, including trading and commercial rights. To hang on to his realm, Liholiho decided that he would need to make a steady show of adopting Western habits. To finance them, he would have to make money, a thing that no Hawaiian ali'i had needed to do before.

Things were changing throughout his reign. The young king had to face overwhelming upheavals the whole time as the life that he had been trained for in childhood when his father was alive ceased to exist, abruptly replaced with a foreign culture that had taken over his home.

How was he going to make money? By selling the sandalwood that grew on the Islands.

The result of this decision, an inevitable one, was that the Hawaiian people were forced to divert their activities from necessary tasks such as farming and fishing and aquaculture to felling sandalwood trees.

As if that weren't enough trouble for Hawaii, savvy foreigners fooled the naïve Hawaiian people and their king about the true value of sandalwood, grossly underpaying them for their precious – and finite – natural resource.

Soon the king had run up horrendous debts to pay for Western trappings, while the diseases of whalers and traders who stopped in Honolulu and Lahaina decimated the native population. Less than half of the Hawaiians who were alive when Liholiho came to power were alive when his reign ended.

It ended because he and Kamamalu took a trip to London, England.

The purpose of the trip had been to follow through on his father's intention of asking the British to make Hawai'i a protectorate, but they both came down with measles before the Hawaiian king could meet with the British king, George IV. Hawaiians, whether ali'i or commoners, who lack prior exposure to the pathogens that the humans on the rest of the planet had been able to build up immunities to, were equally helpless when infected by unfamiliar diseases.

Kamamalu died first. When Liholiho heard about it, he was so upset that he went into a coma and died after six more days. The bodies were brought home by their Hawaiian traveling companions, Boki and Liliha, the governor of O'ahu and his wife. Traditional Hawaiian death rituals were not observed as they had not planned on dying when they went traveling (who does?!), and so had not brought priests on the trip.

Kamehameha III

Kauikeaouli was only eleven years old when he became king. He needed a regent even more than his adult but inexperienced older brother had. He had Queen Kaʻahumanu, and a warrior chief from his father's reign, and others. But Kaʻahumanu died in 1832, when he was seventeen years old – still not ready to rule on his own. His older half-sister, Kinaʻu, took over the role of regent. His wife was Queen Kalama, an intelligent woman who was talented in business and finance. When she died in 1870, she was an independently wealthy woman.

Kinaʻu lived five more years. She was a Christian convert who attended services at the new Kawaiahaʻo Church in Honolulu. There is a stone successor to that church still standing today; the Hawaiian royal family used it for major life events such as marriage and funerals until their rule ended.

Kauikeaouli resisted Christianity while the missionaries promoted it relentlessly, claiming its superiority and citing the technology and strong immune systems of the haoles as proof. The missionaries worked steadily at creating a written form of the Hawaiian language, and after four years of steady effort, succeeded in 1826, less than two years into his reign.

The advent of a written language, along with the schools established by the missionaries, transformed Hawaiian culture. Literacy became universal. Queen Kaʻahumanu set an example for her people by learning to read and write while decreeing that all Hawaiian must do so as well. Soon Hawaiʻi had the highest literacy rate in the world.

Added to the missionaries' efforts for literacy were the schools that they established on each of the Islands where they gained a foothold. Their motive was to spread their own religion and culture among the Hawaiians, but the end result was nonetheless beneficial: literacy, and knowledge of how the haoles thought about the world.

The haoles were both a benefit and a deficit to the young king.

The benefit was that they became useful political advisors to him, including one Dr. Gerrit P. Judd, whose descendant would later become a governor of Hawaiʻi in the early twentieth century, when it was a U.S. territory. Gerrit P. Judd took over when the princess Kinaʻu died in 1839. The king never joined a Christian church, but he made good use of the missionaries.

The deficits were many. So many ships arrived that Hawaiians left with them in droves to try whaling, trading, and whatever else appealed to them, until the king outlawed it, fearful that there would soon be too few Hawaiians living in Hawaii. Not only that, but haole diseases continued to decimate the native population his reign.

The haoles pressured him for the right to establish businesses in Hawaii, to own land for them, and to hire Hawaiians to work in them. This meant stores, ranches, and plantations. The first plantation was on rented land, established in 1835.

One of the missionaries to arrive in Honolulu in 1840 was Daniel Dole, the father of Sanford B. Dole. He went to work at the Punahou School, which was the first one to teach in English.

The king made the most of the benefit of his haole political advisors by getting his realm out of debt and promulgating a constitution in 1840, and then another one in 1852. A legislature was established with a House of Nobles for the aliʻi, Hawaiian males, and select resident haoles were given the right to vote.

A brief crisis developed in 1843 when a British navy commander by the name of George Paulet arrived and forced the king to surrender Hawaiian sovereignty to British control. Five months went by as the British Union Jack flag flew over Hawaiian buildings and lands, until French and American protests brought about a reversal. Rear Admiral Richard Thomas sailed to Hawaiʻi when he found out what Paulet had done, met with the king, got his assurances that British interests in Hawaiʻi would be protected, and that was that…for the time being.

However, aliʻi women had positions on the king's Privy Council, and his father's great-granddaughter, Princess Ruth Keʻelikolani, was appointed as an advisor on it in 1847, when she was 21 years old. Ruth valued traditional Hawaiian culture above haole ways, though she had been taught all about both, and balanced them by wearing Victorian clothing and coiffures while living in a native Hawaiian hale. She later became the governor of the Big Island of Hawaiʻi.

At last in 1848, the king caved to pressure from Dr. Judd and other haoles to divide up feudal lands so that it could all be subject to sale and individual ownership, as it was in other nations. There was the land owned by the king, land owned by the konohiki – the ali'i who were landlords under the king. They wanted a large share of Hawaiian lands for themselves.

The king went first, of course, taking a million acres as his personal property, leaving three million more to divide up. Of those three million, he decreed that half were to become government lands. That left the rest to the konohiki. The royal mahele (division) was the first authority, followed by a confusing new Final Land Commission.

In 1850, kuleana, small land grants of two to three acres, were allowed to Hawaiian commoners who intended to be farmers, but most Hawaiian commoners did not understand land ownership, and lost their grants. These reverted to the crown, which ended up owning half of all Hawaiian land.

Next came the haole businessmen, who found the attitude of common Hawaiians toward land ownership to be odd. Because the haoles were raised to acquire land and make money, they could not understand why Hawaiian people wouldn't be determined to do the same thing. And because the Hawaiians had been raised with a completely different expectation, they did just the opposite of what the haoles did.

A bad thing appeared in Hawai'i in the 1840s, something that caused separations: leprosy.

Leprosy, also known as Hansen's disease, attacks skin, nerves, and bones, causing bones to shrink and nerves to atrophy, leaving no sensation in the affected areas…which, perhaps, is just as well, because over time, the patient's extremities can die and fall off. It starts with skin lesions that don't hurt or show any discharge, and gets worse as time goes on.

Another looming problem that haunted Kamehameha III's administration was the threat of annexation by the United States. The U.S. was in the midst of expanding its territory, having acquired enough of it to stretch from the Atlantic to the Pacific Ocean, and still it wanted more territory. In 1851, there were rumors of adding the nation of Hawai'i.

Hawai'i – Stolen Paradise

A distraction from this issue came in 1853, in the form of a smallpox epidemic, which reduced the total number of native Hawaiians from 150,000 to 70,000.

During this anxious time, in 1852, another constitution was promulgated that limited the king's powers: it required him to share rule with a legislature made up of ali'i and haoles, and to swear an oath to uphold it.

King Kamehameha III and Queen Kalama had had two sons, but both died as infants. This was a common fate among Hawaiians; not only were their numbers being reduced by foreign diseases, but many were unable to have any children at all, or else the ones that they did have were unable to grow to adulthood, reproduce, and raise their own.

The king and queen responded to this personal and political crisis by adopting as hanai children the sons of Queen Kina'u, Alexander Liholiho and Lot Kamehameha. Lot was older, and he was quiet, so it was erroneously assumed that he would be less capable than his brother, who was named as the king's immediate successor.

The king died in 1854 after 30 years of rule, and Alexander Liholiho took his place.

Princess Victoria Kamamalu

The younger sister of Alexander Liholiho and Lot Kamehameha was Hawai'i's first queen.

She was beautiful and, like many of her family, a talented musician.

She was queen for a day – just one day – then her brother took office as Kamehameha IV.

It was never the plan for her to stay in office. She simply found herself there for that much time as kuhina nui (queen regent) presiding over the king's Privy Council, as she had been before her uncle's death. Her brother discontinued the position, and with that, she was out of office.

But that wasn't all that there was to her; Victoria Kamamalu led a very interesting life.

History has overlooked her, but herstory won't.

The princess grew up as close friends and foster sibling to Lili'uokalani, who became queen of Hawaii in 1891. They shared everything together. Her father ended up raising Victoria Kamamalu by himself after her mother, Kina'u, died when she was a year old.

Princess Victoria Kamamalu was betrothed to a distant cousin, William Charles Lunalilo, and she wanted to marry him. The Hawaiian people also approved of the match.

But her brothers were absolutely opposed to it. They didn't want nieces and nephews to be born who would outrank them in mana.

Lunalilo was a closer relative of Kamehameha the Great than they were, and they allowed their jealousy to trump their sister's happiness. Kamehameha IV also persuaded his cousin Lili'uokalani not to marry Lunalilo for the same reason. She ended up marrying the American John Owen Dominis.

Princess Victoria allegedly had an affair with a married Englishman who was a frequent dinner guest of her family, but that ended when her brothers found out and banished him from the Islands.

Princess Victoria Kamamalu thus never married or enjoyed any further professional successes, and died at age 27, single and childless.

Kamehameha IV

Alexander Liholiho did what his predecessors did, and took the official name Kamehameha.

The new king wasted no time in discontinuing all negotiations with the United States about annexation, making it clear that he intended to maintain his nation's sovereignty, not surrender it.

His claim to the throne came from both his lineage and his hanai adoption, and on top of that, he had been formally named heir to the throne by his predecessor. There was thus no difficulty in taking charge at the age of 20. The new king was very handsome, and he had an outgoing demeanor, which made him popular with the people.

Just five years earlier, he and his brother had gone on a trip to the United States, visiting San Francisco and New York, and to Panama and Jamaica, and Europe, to see London and Paris. Dr. Judd had been their chaperone. The trip had two purposes: to show the young princes the outside world, and to negotiate with the French government over a trading dispute. The French refused to meet with Dr. Judd, and the dispute went unresolved until 1853. Meanwhile, he brought the princes home in September of 1850, just two days less than a year since they had left.

Alexander Liholiho had a good time in London. He was particularly enamored of British royalty and its trappings of prestige. However, he did not have as a good a time in the U.S., where he had an unpleasant experience with racial prejudice.

Regardless, the trip left him with more of a Western bent than that of his predecessors, neither of whom had been raised with such a background. For Kamehameha IV, things Western were part of his background and experience, which shaped his view of the world, and affected his attitudes and decisions.

When he returned home, he was given a place on his uncle the king's Privy Council, which he held until his brother's death three years later. As a result, he had some valuable political experience under his belt when he became king.

The new king discontinued the position of queen regent and relied on his haole advisors, all of whom had been required to swear oaths of loyalty to the Hawaiian king and to Hawai'i long ago in order to serve in government there. He appointed Prince Lot as general in command of Hawai'i's military.

The first piece of advice that the new king received was that he ought to get married so that he could produce an heir, thus providing continuity and stability to the Kamehameha dynasty. Accordingly, he asked his childhood sweetheart, whom he had known since his days at the Chiefs' Children's School in Honolulu.

Emma Naea Rooke was the granddaughter of John Young, the scout whom Kamehameha the Great had kidnapped and co-opted as one of his two haole advisors. She was also a distant cousin and a princess, someone whom the missionaries could not object to. Like her fiancé, she too had been adopted as a hanai child. The two were married on June 19, 1856. He was 22, she was 21, and they were very happy together.

The king attempted to replace the constitution of 1852, but was unsuccessful.

The whaling industry took off during Kamehameha IV's reign, and gas lighting came to Honolulu in 1859. In 1860, a steamship called the *Kilauea* went into service as an inter-island transport, considerably shortening the time it took to travel between the Islands.

King Kamehameha IV and Queen Emma founded an Episcopalian chapel in Hawai'i, in contrast to his predecessor, who had had no interest in foreign religion. The Hawaiian people were not delighted about this.

After nearly two years, a prince was born to the couple, and he was named Albert Edward Kauikeaouli Leiopapa. Queen Victoria and her husband Prince Albert agreed to be his absent godparents. He was to be his parents' only child.

Unfortunately, he didn't live to grow up and have children himself. When he was four years old, in 1862, he died after a brief illness. The illness was likely brought on by a seizure that was not recognized as such, but instead treated as an out-of-control tantrum, then aggravated by his father dousing the boy with ice-cold water. That left the king with a lasting sense of guilt.

Kamehameha IV

Just over two years earlier, Alexander Liholiho had mistakenly believed that his personal secretary, an American named Henry Neilson, was having an affair with Queen Emma. Before the king realized that it wasn't true, he shot his friend in the stomach. The king rushed to get medical help. Neilson lived in discomfort for two and a half more years, and then he died.

The king had already been feeling guilty over the death of his friend, which was quite obviously his fault, and now he was convinced that he was the cause of the death of his only child. His friend and his son died one right after the other, in 1861 and 1862.

The king's health deteriorated rapidly, and he became more and more religious. He had chronic asthma, lost the will to live, and died at the age of twenty-nine, after nine years of rule.

Queen Emma was devastated. She never remarried.

Kamehameha V

Lot Kapuaiwa became king when his brother died with no heir, and died without leaving one.

He had hoped to marry the princess Bernice Pauahi, but she chose to marry a haole man named Charles Reed Bishop in 1850. Princess Bernice was happy with Bishop, an American who became a naturalized Hawaiian citizen and a banker. They had no children. She was determined to learn as much as she could about haole culture by immersing herself in it. Marrying into it and living as one of them seemed like an effective method of doing that.

Lot didn't get over it, nor did he make up his mind to marry someone else and leave an heir.

He did name his younger sister, the princess Victoria Kamamalu, as his heir, but she died.

With that plan nixed by fate, Lot still needed to settle upon a willing fiancée.

Instead, he found himself in love with his sister-in-law, Queen Emma. That was a futile emotion as well; she was devoted to her husband's memory and not interested in him.

Unlike his younger brother, Lot was not handsome or charismatic. He was a very calm and quiet man, and he took office without complaint, inspiring confidence with his demeanor, measured reasoning, and self-assurance.

Lot also had no great love for foreign ways, preferring traditional Hawaiian customs and beliefs. He did dress in a European-style military outfit, and he did not attempt to undo each and every foreign change that had come to Hawaii, but he was not interested in adding to them.

Lot ended up ruling for as many years as his brother had – nine.

When he took office, he was asked to swear an oath to the 1852 constitution. He refused.

Kamehameha V

The haole Cabinet thought that amendments would be made to that document, and that it would continue in service, but Lot had other ideas.

In July of 1864, he called a constitutional convention to discuss the details of a new document, focusing on a provision concerning voting rights. It limited the vote to residents who could pass a literacy test (no one objected to that) and to those males who either owned property or earned a certain level of income.

The agreement broke down as the delegates looped into a series of debates, so Lot dismissed the meeting and said he would give them a constitution. He did exactly that on August 20, 1864, signed it into law, and that was that. The Hawaiian king now had many of the original powers of office back, with those of the Privy Council scaled back, and those of the king and Cabinet in a dominant role. Lot toured the Islands to meet the people and spread the news of the new constitution, which was well-received.

During Lot's reign, two significant historical events took place: one was the sale of the island of Ni'ihau, and the other was the escalation of the isolation of Hawaiians suffering from leprosy.

In 1864, he allowed the sale of the entire island of Ni'ihau to Elizabeth Sinclair for the sum of $10,000 in gold. Her daughter, Helen, had married one Charles B. Robinson, and they inherited the island from her. The Robinson family was based on Kauai, but frequently traveled the short distance of just a few hours by sail or rowboat to Ni'ihau. The people of Ni'ihau thought of the widow Sinclair as their chiefess.

To the present day, the island of Ni'ihau is known as the Forbidden Island, and visits are by invitation only. Each visitor is checked for indications of pathogens that could attack the immune systems of the residents, who speak only their own dialect of the Hawaiian language. They have had no contact with the pathogens that outsiders have built natural immunities to.

The Robinson family still owns the island. They pay astronomical sums in taxes to the United States government each year to keep things as they are. But…there are only two childless cousins left. Hopefully, the people of Ni'ihau will be left alone.

Hawai'i – Stolen Paradise

To prevent contagion, a leper colony was established in 1865 on the northern side of the island of Moloka'i. At first, patients could be visited by their relatives, but eight years later the colony was put into total quarantine, isolated from anyone and everyone who was not infected. Scientists have since determined that 95 percent of humans are immune to leprosy.

It made no difference who showed the early signs of the disease – there were no exceptions, no exemptions, and no redemptions. A commoner or a musical celebrity or an ali'i could all be sent there for life, with only a brief glimpse of their relatives waving good-bye to them at the pier as they boarded the boat. A member of the Privy Council was found to be infected; he was banished for life to Moloka'i. In just 3 years, 8,000 Hawaiians were sent there. Being sent there must have felt like the end of the world, with no contact with one's family allowed ever again.

Meanwhile, the sons of the missionaries had grown up. They had no interest in a religious life. They wanted to make money, and they were very busy doing so, dominating many aspects of economic, social, and political life in Hawai'i.

Sugar plantations (over 30 of them), pineapple plantations, inter-island transportation companies, utility companies that offered gas lighting and electricity, and shipping companies that ferried goods to and from the Islands flourished. Haoles from America, England, France, and Germany became wealthy, and they wanted more, and more, and more.

As a result, the haoles were bringing in more and more outside help to labor cheaply on their plantations or in their other businesses, from China, then from Japan, and later from Portugal. Soon there were many more foreigners living on the Islands than there were Hawaiians. The total number of native Hawaiians during Lot's reign was estimated to be around 60,000.

Whaling was a waning industry thanks to the discovery of petroleum oil in Pennsylvania.

In 1866, Mark Twain visited the Islands, touring O'ahu, Mau'i, and the Big Island of Hawai'i. He was a journalist then, not a famous author yet, with no published books out. He came to write articles for a Sacramento newspaper, the *Union*, and he managed to stretch his visit

Kamehameha V

out to far longer than the time agreed upon by his employer. He paid the newspaper back with plenty of letters for publication. He saw Kilauea, smelled coconut oil on native women, and observed that Hawaiʻi "had more missionaries…than would take to convert hell itself."

A hotel was built in 1872, the first of many. It was a huge, rambling, Victorian building, painted pink, called the Royal Hawaiian Hotel, and it had the approval of the king. It was the first of many.

As for King Lot Kamehameha, he had the palace that his brother had ordered built, Aliʻiolani Hale, designated an administrative building instead of a royal residence due to fiscal concerns. Today it houses the judicial branch of Hawaiʻi's state government, and faces ʻIolani Palace.

However, he also had a royal barracks built, a quarantine house for immigrants, a prison, an insane asylum, and the Royal Mausoleum.

When he died (of morbid obesity) in December of 1872, he left a nation heavily in debt.

His efforts to name a successor had not produced a new monarch, either.

He had attempted to name Princess Bernice Pauahi Bishop as his heir, but she said no.

A crisis over the end of the Kamehameha dynasty ensued as a replacement was sought.

Lunalilo Rules for Over a Year

With the death of the last Kamehameha, Hawai'i had to look to another branch of the ali'i families for a new king or queen, and one who was as closely related to Kamehameha the Great as possible was desired.

The 1864 constitution decreed that the king could name his successor, and that the House of Nobles would have to confirm that individual. But Lot hadn't been able to follow through on that, so the legislature had to decide. The Cabinet scheduled a January 1873 meeting.

The choices were: 1. Prince William Charles Lunalilo, who was most closely related; 2. Princess Ruth Ke'elikolani, the dead king's half-sister, a great-granddaughter of Kamehameha the Great, and experienced governess of the Big Island of Hawai'i, who kept to traditional Hawaiian ways, choosing to speak the Hawaiian language even though she understood English; 3. David Kalakaua, a lawyer who was descended from the ali'i warriors of Kona on the Big Island who had supported Kamehameha the Great; and 4. Princess Bernice Pauahi Bishop, a great-granddaughter of Kamehameha the Great.

Bernice didn't want the job – so she was out of the running.

Ruth Ke'elikolani was considered too traditional for it – out also.

That brought it down to the two men.

They campaigned for the post for the remainder of December 1872, and Lunalilo won.

Kalakaua accepted his defeat gracefully. Lunalilo appointed a Cabinet of one Scot and the rest Americans, which included Princess Bernice's husband, the banker Charles Reed Bishop, and an attorney named A. Francis Judd. He was the son of Dr. Gerrit P. Judd.

Lunalilo had strong American preferences, democratic beliefs, and he enjoyed drinking. The Hawaiian people liked him, and he walked barefoot to Kawaiaha'o Church to take his oath of office. Thousands of Hawaiians cheered him on.

Lunalilo Rules for Over a Year

During Lunalilo's reign, there were some further developments concerning leprosy.

A Belgian priest by the name of Father Damien arrival in Honolulu in 1864. He was soon assigned to the Big Island of Hawai'i, where he remained until his bishop asked for volunteers to go to the leper colony. The year was 1873. The bishop didn't want to order anyone to go, because he was certain that they would catch leprosy and die horribly. But four priests volunteered, and Father Damien was the first one, which is why history remembers him so well.

A year later, Father Damien noticed the early signs of the disease.

He is believed to contracted leprosy by sharing poi with others at mealtimes, perhaps to make the patients feel less emotional isolation. Poi, a paste made of pulverized and cooked taro, a starch vegetable, is served in dishes and eaten by dipping one's finger in, then licking the poi off. With multiple eaters sharing the same dish of poi in this way, anyone not infected but also among the unfortunate five percent who are not genetically immune will contract leprosy.

Father Damien died of the dreaded disease after ten years, in 1884. He accepted his fate calmly, and allowed himself to be photographed while suffering from leprosy but still able to work, and again on his deathbed. He was forty-nine years old when he died.

Aside from this, two issues figured most prominently in his reign – two related issues.

Both concerned the United States. One issue was that of sugar: the Hawaiian government wanted a reciprocity treaty, so that sugar could enter the U.S. duty-free. The other had to do with Pearl Harbor: the U.S. wanted to use it as a port for its naval vessels.

This set the stage for a quid pro quo deal…until the Hawaiian people protested and the issue was left unresolved for the time being.

A harsh Hungarian commander, Joseph Jajczay, had been hired to direct the Royal Household Troops, and they mutinied, fed up with him. They wanted him removed, along with Charles H. Judd, the adjutant general.

Hawai'i – Stolen Paradise

This crisis was only resolved when the king, suffering from tuberculosis after a lifetime of drinking, pleaded with them to stop. He ended up disbanding them, leaving only the Royal Hawaiian Band.

Lunalilo did not marry or produce an heir.

The woman he had wanted, the sister of his predecessor, had died.

He had been insulted by his would-be brothers-in-law as they jealously guarded their own positions as top mana-wielders, and he was still angry about that.

As a result, when he died at the age of 39 of pneumonia and tuberculosis in early February of 1874, he left instructions that he was not to be interred in the Royal Mausoleum with them.

His father had a small mausoleum built just for him next to Kawaiaha'o Church.

A Hotly Contested Election

This time, the candidates were David Kalakaua, Queen Emma, and Bernice Pauahi Bishop.

Once again, Princess Bernice Pauahi made it clear that she did not want to be queen.

That was an unfortunate decision for a couple of reasons. One was that when Princess Ruth Ke'elikolani died, she left all of her property to Bernice, which made her the wealthiest person in Hawai'i, in possession of one-ninth of Hawaiian lands. The other was her lineage. As a great-granddaughter of Kamehameha the Great, she would have been ideal for the job, having the highest mana in the nation.

A portrait of Princess Bernice Pauahi Bishop by Jennie S. Loop that hangs in her museum.

But no, she didn't want to be queen, even though she got along well with haoles and Hawaiians alike, and was well-respected by all. She understood both Hawaiian and Anglo-American culture completely, so this was a disappointment.

Hawai'i – Stolen Paradise

Princess Bernice Pauahi lived until 1884, and Charles R. Bishop opened the museum in her honor in 1891. It houses the largest collection of Polynesian artifacts in the Pacific.

Queen Emma, the widow of Kamehameha IV, ran against Kalakaua, but lost. She never spoke to him again, or his wife, despite having to attend many events that ali'i were expected to appear at. Kalakaua and Kapi'olani, however, behaved politely to her.

When she lost the election, a huge riot by her Hawaiian supporters ensued, prompting Kalakaua to allow the troops on board 3 military ships anchored in Pearl Harbor, 2 American and 1 British, to put it down. This set a disturbing precedent for his reign, not that he had much choice when faced with such a disturbance. One man was thrown out of an upper-story window. He later died from his injuries.

Queen Emma kept track of politics in Hawai'i for the rest of her life, deeply concerned by the possibility that it might someday become a part of the United States. She died at the age of 49, in 1885, having founded a hospital for her people, whose numbers continued to dwindle.

The Merrie Monarch

King Kalakaua's reign is memorable for both a spectacular success and a disastrous failure.

His success was in reviving Hawaiian culture, and he immediately went to work doing that after his election to the throne in 1874. Kalakaua became known as the Merrie Monarch, because he restored the practice of hula dancing to Hawaiian culture. He had it performed at his coronation ceremony. That was held in 1883, after a new 'Iolani Palace was completed in 1879, to replace the older, much smaller hale (house) that had been infested with termites.

Kalakaua revived surfing and lua, the martial art of Hawai'i. He and his sisters and brother were great songwriters; they wrote music and lyrics, and his *Hawai'i Pono'i* is now the state song of Hawai'i. He also commissioned the statue of Kamehameha the Great in his traditional attire and feather helmet, which stands across the street from the Palace, in front of what is now a judicial building.

He traveled extensively to establish Hawai'i as a nation in the minds of other reigning monarchs and heads of state, visiting Japan, Siam, and other countries in Asia and Southeast Asia. King Kalakaua was the first reigning monarch of any country to travel the world, and to visit the United States.

This statue of Kamehameha the Great in his traditional warrior attire as a strong, active, young warrior was cast by the artist Thomas Ridgeway Gould in 1880 and installed in 1883, the year of Kalakaua's coronation. It stands in front of Ali'iolani Hale, Hawai'i's judicial and legislative building, and it faces 'Iolani Palace.

Hawai'i – Stolen Paradise

Kalakaua hosted Robert Louis Stevenson on his boathouse in Pearl Harbor, and showed himself to be an amiable host to each visitor to the Islands. He was determined to show the outside world through pomp and circumstance that Hawai'i was as advanced and current with world events and practices as any other country.

His failure was political and financial.

He spent a lot of money doing this, and put his country $2 million in debt to a wealthy man from California by the name of Claus Spreckels by 1886, but later paid him off by borrowing from others.

Kalakaua left his sister, Lili'uokalani, in charge when he was away. While he was traveling in 1881, a ship arrived at Pearl Harbor with goods from China...and smallpox. Lili'uokalani responded by promptly closing the port, because smallpox typically decimated the native Hawaiian population.

That did not sit well with the sons of the missionaries, who by now were wealthy from sugar and pineapple plantations, and from shipping and transportation. They ultimately became known to history as the Big Five – representing five wealthy and powerful corporate interests in Hawai'i. They protested that they needed (!) to make money without the slightest interruption; they did not care about the native people, only their wallets. Lili'uokalani replied that her first duty was to her people; she didn't care right back.

Things reached a breaking point over the nation's finances and the king's efforts to promote Hawaiian security for Hawaiians, both present and future. Although the haole ministers whom each king appointed had long been required to swear an oath of loyalty to Hawaii and to the king or queen, a secret coup was being planned.

A secret political organization called the Hawaiian League was formed. It was made up of non-native citizens of Hawaii and haoles, and led by a group of men who called themselves the Committee of Thirteen. This group allied itself with three companies of the Honolulu Rifles. The individuals in those groups were all non-native volunteers.

In 1887, at bayonet-point, the Big Five forced King David Kalakaua to accept a new constitution that practically eviscerated his own political powers. It also required that one own property in order to vote, which disenfranchised native Hawai'ians, as it was only the ali'i

The Merrie Monarch

who actually held title to any. Haoles had been allowed to buy property for quite some time, and they had used it to amass wealth and to gain footholds as advisors to the royal family, with the consequence that many white men held prominent positions in the national legislature and the king's Cabinet.

That was the same year that the king sent his wife and sister to represent Hawaii in London at Queen Victoria's Golden Jubilee celebration. They weren't home for the events of the Bayonet Constitution. Instead, they traveled by boat to San Francisco, then across the United States to Washington, D.C., up to New York City, and by boat again to London, England.

Queen Kapi'olani had her gown made up in Manhattan. It was fabulous, with beautiful peacock feathers sewn into it. Princess Lili'uokalani had something spectacular to wear, too: a butterfly pin made of diamonds to wear in her hair. The wings were separate pieces with springs behind them, so that the butterfly appeared to flutter as she walked. The two ali'i women were treated with as much respect as any visiting royalty in London, and Queen Victoria gave them a private meeting.

This photograph of Princess Lili'uokalani with Queen Kapi'olani is on a stand in the queen's sitting room in 'Iolani Palace. It shows them at the Golden Jubilee celebration for Queen Victoria in London, England in 1887. Note the peacock feathers in the queen's gown, and the diamond butterfly pin in Lili'uokalani's hair.

Hawai'i – Stolen Paradise

Kalakaua and his wife, Queen Kapi'olani had no children, so his sister, Lili'uokalani, was next in line to the throne. But his sister and her husband, John Owen Dominis, who had emigrated to Hawaii from Boston, Massachusetts, had not had any children either. So, next in line came their niece, the daughter of their dead sister, Princess Likelike, and her Scottish husband, Archibald Scott Cleghorn. Her name was Princess Victoria Ka'iulani Cleghorn, and her aunt named her as heir to the throne when she became Queen of Hawai'i.

Princess Ka'iulani

It's funny how movies often sacrifice historical accuracy for drama. A case in point is that of *Princess Ka'iulani*. In it, when the bayonets came out in 1887, the widowed Cleghorn grabbed his teenage daughter and took her away to attend boarding school in Britain for several years. She was very upset to leave her home, which she loved and was the only place she knew, but her aunt and uncle could hardly have wished her to stay for that. She came back an educated, eloquent young woman, but to the devastating news that her country had been lost.

The movie evoked great sympathy for the princess and, for me, interest.

What actually happened was a bit more drawn out. Ka'iulani didn't go away to school until a couple of years after her uncle was bullied into accepting that constitution. When she did go, it was well-planned and publicized, and her father went with her as far as San Francisco. There was no hurry or anxiety to it, only a fond farewell with lei and ceremony to it. She went the rest of the way to school with a chaperone. Of course, a movie showing her dad grabbing a kicking, crying, objecting teenager and carrying her away from gunfire is much more exciting to watch...

The princess did come back when she was in her early twenties, several years later.

Princess Victoria Kawekiu Lunalilo Kalaninuiahilapalapa Ka'iulani Cleghorn was the niece of King David Kalakaua and of his sister and successor, Queen Lili'uokalani. The princess was the heir to the Hawaiian throne. Ka'iulani grew up preparing herself for her future role as queen of Hawai'i, but by the time she was an adult, the Big Five had stolen her country, and she was broken-hearted. Today, there is a statue of her with one of her pet peacocks where her estate once was, in Waikiki, three blocks south of the Ala Wai Canal.

Princess Ka'iulani's mother was Kalakaua and Lili'uokalani's sister, Princess Miriam Likelike, a vivacious beauty with a temper that overpowered her only daughter's until her death, when Ka'iulani was eleven years old. Ka'iulani was raised with servants, a nanny, and then governesses on her parents' estate at Waikiki, 'Ainahau.

Hawai'i – Stolen Paradise

Her mother had named it; 'Ainahau means "cool place" – a cool breeze from Manoa Valley to the north comes through it. Her aunt, the governess of the Big Island of Hawai'i, Princess Ruth Ke'elikolani, had made a gift of the land to her new niece when she was born.

Her father, Archibald Cleghorn, was a Scot who had come to the island with his dying father at age sixteen and stayed to make his fortune. He had three daughters (Rose, Helen, and Annie) with a Hawaiian woman, was widowed, and then married Princess Likelike after that. Cleghorn became a Hawaiian citizen the same year that he married the princess, and their daughter knew and visited often with her half-sisters.

The family lived on Queen Emma Street when Ka'iulani was born on October 16, 1875. They attended St. Andrew's Episcopal Church, except when larger ceremonies involved their extended family of relatives. For those, they would go to Kawaiaha'o Church, which is just a short walk away from 'Iolani Palace, in Honolulu. At that time, Ka'iulani's parents were having a new home built on 'Ainahau, within sight of Waikiki Beach.

'Ainahau was a paradise to the princess when she was a little girl. She had a fabulous banyan tree close to the house. When the famous writer and poet Robert Louis Stevenson – known as Tusitala to the Tahitians, or "teller of tales" – made the first of two visits to Hawai'i, he was staying across the street from 'Ainahau. Ka'iulani was allowed to go and visited him there, and he visited her under her tree. Stevenson wrote her a poem about it when their weeks together were ending. She was going to school in Britain, and she would leave the Islands before he did.

An 'Ohai-ali'i plant in bloom at Foster Botanical Garden. This dragon-like blossom grew all over 'Ainahau when Princess Ka'iulani lived there.

But before that, she enjoyed about ten years on her estate, swimming the waters off Waikiki Beach, riding her pony, and enjoying the breezes under date palms and the cinnamon, teak, and cypress trees that grew there, and eating mangos on other trees at 'Ainahau. She spent her free time admiring hibiscus blossoms, and inhaling the scent of her favorite flower, jasmine, which grew everywhere she looked.

Peacocks always walked on the grounds. They were Ka'iulani's pets, she loved to feed them.

Her father had built an artesian well just for the three lily ponds, and one of them was built in the shape of a shamrock. A traditional, one-room Hawaiian hale was left on the estate as a garden house, but with a modern wooden floor and furniture added. Everything was a mixture of Ka'iulani's two backgrounds, Hawaiian and Scottish.

She was home-schooled at the estate after being raised by a nurse, May Leleo. Her governesses were a Miss Barnes and then an American, a Miss Gardinier, who left her post to get married. It was Miss Gardinier who did Ka'iulani a great favor: she insisted upon obedience and politeness. Princess Likelike realized this was the right thing to do, as it would teach her daughter to be a good leader later in life.

Whenever she went out in her family's carriage, Ka'iulani was taught to smile and wave, not to just ride comfortably and lapse into her own thoughts. She had to put on a public face of greeting to her people, who were happy at the chance to catch sight of her.

When Ka'iulani was eleven years old, she lost her mother.

Princess Miriam Likelike died a mysterious death. Native Hawaiians believed that she had been prayed to death by a kahuna priest. No doubt, there is a scientific explanation, but she appeared to lose her will to live and she stopped eating. Nothing helped, and she declined gradually over the course of a year and three months.

Traditional Hawaiian beliefs were invoked for the princess's illness again as the end drew near. The volcano Mauna Loa was erupting on the Big Island of Hawai'i, and a school of red akule fish had been seen in the waters offshore there. These had always been omens that an ali'i would die soon.

Hawai'i – Stolen Paradise

Just before she died, she told her daughter that she could see her future: she would go away for a long time, never marry, and never be queen. Ka'iulani ran from her mother's room to talk to Miss Gardinier, very upset.

Princess Ka'iulani left Hawai'i as a teenager to attend school in England before her uncle was forced to sign away most of his political powers. She walked up the gangplank of the ship that was take her as far as San Francisco on May 10, 1889, wearing a farewell lei from her former governess, who had come to see her off. The Royal Hawaiian Band played her uncle Papa Moi's *Hawai'i Pono'i* in her honor.

Her country went through many changes while she was away, and by the time she came home in 1897, she was no longer heir to the throne, only a princess without the purpose that she had studied for. She returned to her home by way of New York City and Washington, D.C. after pleading her country's case with the U.S. president and the press, to no avail.

Princess Ka'iulani had gone to see President Grover Cleveland and the First Lady, Frances Folsom Cleveland, on her way home to Hawai'i, and begged for his help. But when Ka'iulani met Cleveland, it was 1897. Cleveland was on his way out of office after his second and final term, and he had been out of office for one term – 4 years – while his political rival, a Republican named Benjamin Harrison, was president.

The annexation talks had resumed during that time. Now, as he was leaving again and another Republican, William McKinley, was taking his place, the annexation talks had resumed. He could do little more than greet Ka'iulani pleasantly, promise her nothing more than good wishes, and say good-bye.

It was 1897 when Ka'iulani finally headed home. Her education was complete, and she realized that there was no reason to delay, or to wait to be summoned home. Her absence was pointless. She had stayed away at first for the sake of her education, then to avoid causing distraction when the attention was meant to be on her aunt, and still longer when she attempted to help by traveling in the United States and being seen as a dignified, poised lady who would either rule capably or get along with others, depending on the situation.

Princess Ka'iulani

When she got home, her father showed her what he had done at 'Ainahau in anticipation of her reign as Hawaii's queen, which was a sad tour knowing that now Ka'iulani would be simply an ali'i lady who cordially received visitors.

Archibald Cleghorn had worked very hard to surprise his daughter with a whole new Victorian-style mansion, complete with a suite of rooms upstairs for her to sleep and write in, and a kahili-coronet motif on the high ceiling. A huge drawing room below befitted an heiress to a throne that she would not occupy, and a wide lanai wrapped around the outside of the new house.

The princess went to visit her aunt, Mama Moi, the widowed Queen Kapi'olani, who had made her cousins, the princes David Kawananakoa and Kuhio her hanai sons. They lived with her. The drawing room had an enormous, fabulous feather kahili in the center.

After making the rounds of greeting her family, an endless series of receptions ensued for callers and well-wishers who trouped through her drawing room at 'Ainahau, followed by social event after social event. Ka'iulani smiled graciously through it all, not saying a word about politics or her situation.

Portrait of Princess Kaiulani, taken by an unknown photographer. Kahili Room, Bernice Pauahi Bishop Museum.

The only political statement she made was done without words, along with her aunt, the deposed Queen Lili'uokalani, and her cousins Kuhio and Koa. They boycotted the annexation ceremony and celebrations in Honolulu, staying away from it all at Washington Place.

Hawai'i – Stolen Paradise

In 1898, her cousin, Prince David Kawananakoa, announced their engagement.

But Ka'iulani never got over the loss of her country, and her grief wasn't about the loss of a throne. To her, the throne was a means for looking after the welfare of the Hawaiian people, so its loss meant that she could not do that anymore. After being raised and educated with that expectation in mind, she found it devastating.

Depressed, and with her immune system compromised by a change in climate – by moving home from years away in Britain – she had difficulty adjusting. She visited the Big Island and went horseback riding in Kona, where her godmother, the six-foot-tall Princess Ruth, had served as governor. The Big Island of Hawai'i has thirteen microclimates, and the mountains of Kona have frequent rainfalls. It had been years since Ka'iulani had been there, years since she and her mother had visited her aunt. Both women were dead, and Ka'iulani was twenty-three years old. She got caught in a rain that was more mist than rain.

Soon she was soaked, and Ka'iulani wore the fashions of late Victorian times. It was 1899, which meant that she wore several petticoats, a corset, and a bodice with an overskirt and underskirt on top of all that. The weight of women's attire in the late nineteenth century tended toward eighty pounds. She had not worn the raincoat that had been provided for her. The princess went back to her hosts' home, and was soon ill.

Her father came to get her. He brought her back to 'Ainahau, where she lay sick in her room for a month and a half. Ka'iulani lived in her room, visited constantly by her father, waited on by the household staff, while reports on her condition were published in local papers. She died at 2 a.m. in her room at 'Ainahau at the age of twenty-three on March 6, 1899.

Her flock of pet peacocks, on the lawn below her window, all screamed at once at that moment.

Today 'Ainahau is part of Honolulu, which has sprawled to encompass and incorporate 'Ainahau as it expanded from the area that surrounded 'Iolani Palace in the late nineteenth century to a much larger municipality.

Princess Kaʻiulani

On Kalakaua Avenue, which runs along the coast of the former estate, including Hermes of Paris, Bulgari, a large Apple computer store, hotels, and restaurants. The Ala Wai Canal runs parallel to Kalakaua Avenue to its northeast. In between them is a neighborhood of streets and avenues named for the members of her family – cousins, parents, aunts, uncles, and so on. Small apartment buildings, low-rise, low-budget hotels, and parking areas now occupy the land that her childhood estate once occupied.

In the midst of all that sits a small triangular park with benches, palm trees, plumeria trees, grass, trash cans, and recycle bins. The park is bordered by Kuhio Avenue, Kanakepolei Street, and Kaiulani Avenue. Traffic consisting of cars, buses, and taxis rush noisily past and around it. Little notice to this park, or to what is in it, is paid by the occupants of those vehicles.

In that park is a tall, black statue of Princess Kaʻiulani with one of her pet peacocks.

This bronze statue of the princess was created by sculptor Jan Gordon Fisher, and unveiled on her 124th birthday, October 16, 1999.

However, the princess is visited as she stands there, frozen in the act of feeding her pet. When I got there, it was a Sunday afternoon. The statue was draped with lei made of orange ilima flowers and pink-and-white orchids, and of long green leaves artfully woven together. Hawaiians have not forgotten her, and they still appreciate her.

Her house is gone, torn down in 1955, and replaced by a hotel: the Sheraton Princess Ka'iulani. It was built by the Matson Navigation Company, and it is a huge, sprawling, commercial property with all of the things that the Big Five would approve of: a swimming pool, an exercise room, conference rooms, and so on. South of that, across Kalakaua Avenue, with its back to Waikiki Beach, is the Moana Hotel, which was completed at the end of Ka'iulani's life. It is a large, symmetrical, Victorian structure, painted white. It opened in 1901; the website is:

http://www.moana-surfrider.com/propertyoverview/hotelhistory/

A Reciprocity Treaty

There was something that the haole population wanted very much by the time of King Kamehameha IV's reign: a treaty with the United States that would allow sugar and molasses from Hawai'i to enter duty-free in return for the right to keep a U.S. Navy depot and dry dock in Pearl Harbor. This was referred to as a reciprocity treaty.

Twenty years of discussion ensued, during which time the Hawaiian rulers postponed the idea. Three kings later, the issue was still being pushed. Neither Kalakaua nor his sister and successor, Lili'uokalani, were in favor of it.

The ali'i siblings thought of the idea of a reciprocity treaty as a slippery slope that would lead to a loss of sovereignty over Pearl Harbor. However, after relentless pressure, Kalakaua finally agreed to have the treaty drafted. In September of 1876, the U.S. Congress approved it.

Kalakaua Returns One Last Time

Kalakaua's health had been deteriorating under the stresses that he was under from the haoles, from the ever-increasing financial pressures on his government, and from the attacks on his sovereignty. He decided to travel in the United States again, but had died while doing so in 1891, and his sister had ascended to the throne.

The Hawaiian people had been preparing celebrations to welcome him home, and the colorful decorations that they had put up were hastily covered with black as the ship carrying Kalakaua appeared on the horizon, also draped in black.

Queen Liliʻuokalani

Liliʻuokalani was a talented songwriter, just as her brothers and sister had been; she wrote one of most the famous songs of Hawaiʻi, *Aloha ʻOʻe*. She was a tall, large woman with a pretty face and regal bearing, and she had no problem assuming political authority when it befell her.

The queen was a highly accomplished musician and composer. She could play the organ, which she did at Kawaiahaʻo Church nearby. She also played the piano, the guitar, the ʻukulele, and the zither. She was a prolific writer of music and lyrics, and she even taught music. A talent for and strong love of music was ingrained in her culture and in her family.

Liliʻuokalani still lived across the street from ʻIolani Palace, in Washington Place, where she had moved upon her marriage to John Owen Dominis. She preferred to live there, across from the back yard of ʻIolani Palace. That was where she had lived since marrying her childhood friend, John Owen Dominis in 1862.

The house is still there. It is a white painted structure with a porte-cochère, a yard with a garden around the house and the walled perimeter, and lots of palm trees with a curved driveway sweeping across the front of it. Today, it is a National Historic Landmark, protected from use and shown by appointment only. The governor's mansion is right behind it.

Washington Place, the home of Queen Liliʻuokalani, on Beretania Street behind ʻIolani Palace.

Hawai'i – Stolen Paradise

Washington Place is a large white mansion at 320 Beretania Street. It was built in 1844, when Captain John Dominis came to Hawai'i with his wife, Mary Jones Dominis and their son, John Owen Dominis. (They had two daughters whom they had left in boarding school in upstate New York, but both of them died young before ever coming to Hawai'i.) Captain Dominis wanted to buy nice furnishings for the house, so he kept taking off on long voyages, and was lost at sea two years later, leaving his wife and 14-year-old son alone there.

Just inside the fence of Washington Place is a large rock with a bronze plaque in it. The rock is lying in the bright sunshine, tilted a bit, facing the sky.

The plaque has a profile of Queen Lili'uokalani at the top, with a *maile lei* of green leaves just under it, not tied together in a loop but hanging open, as per tradition. The border is flowers, and it reminded me of a lei of 'ohai-ali'i flowers. Inside all that is the queen's song, both in musical notes at the top and in lyrics below, *Aloha 'Oe*.

John attended a day school that was right next door to the Royal School, which was the one that the Hawaiian ali'i children attended. He used to climb the fence and chat with them, and he soon became friends with many of them, including the Princess Liliʻu, who later became known as Liliʻuokalani. She was six years younger than her future husband.

When the princess was 24 years old and John O. Dominis was 30, they were married, and she came to live with her husband and mother-in-law at Washington Place. After that, Liliʻuokalani lived there for the rest of her life with only brief exceptions: travel to other islands, travel to the United States and Europe, brief stays at Waikiki Beach, where she had another home, and her imprisonment at ʻIolani Palace when royalists tried to restore her to the Hawaiian throne.

Her mother-in-law wasn't happy to have a non-Caucasian daughter-in-law, and the princess, like many other aliʻi, wanted children but couldn't have any. This meant that she wasn't happy living there until her mother-in-law was a lot older. By that time, the two women were used to one another and the mother-in-law had become more accepting of the princess. Gradually, the two woman had adjusted to one another. Meanwhile, her husband became her friend and political advisor.

Her husband didn't spend a lot of time with her, but he was still a friend to her, and she valued and depended upon his advice while he was alive. John Owen Dominis was the governor of Oahu from 1868 until his death in 1891, several months after his wife became queen. He had a son by another woman, and the queen adopted him according to Hawaiian custom, making him her hanai in 1910. The son was born in 1883, his name was John Dominis ʻAimoku, and his mother was one of her maids. She changed his name to John ʻAimoku Dominis at that time. He lived at Washington Place with the queen until she died in 1917, then moved out with his wife and children.

That was nice; at least she had someone she liked to keep her company. The queen wrote in her autobiography that her husband had been making some changes to the house to surprise her when she returned from her tour of the Islands during the summer of 1891. It was a tradition for a new Hawaiian monarch to tour the Islands to meet the Hawaiian people and be seen by them shortly after taking the throne, so Liliuokalani had spent part of the summer doing that.

What an awful homecoming, to find her husband on his deathbed when she got back! Losing him in September of 1891 doubly hard for

Lili'uokalani. He had been the governor of O'ahu from 1868 until his death. She appointed Princess Ka'iulani's father, Archibald Cleghorn, to the post.

Even though she was upset by this loss, Lili'uokalani forged on, determined to work on behalf of her people and to get back the political rights that her brother had lost during his reign. She wanted a Cabinet that would vote favorably on measures that she intended to pass, and she wanted a legal system that would not require her to get approval from the cabinet on every act that she chose to sign into law.

To get that, she had to dismiss a few Cabinets before she had one that she was satisfied would be sufficiently loyal to her, and cooperate with her agenda. That took two years. Meanwhile, the queen learned the administrative basics of running the country from Honolulu, then spent her first spring and summer in office doing the traditional royal tour of the Islands to greet her people, only to come home to find her husband dying.

Added to those problems was the fact that of the total human population residing on the Islands, only slightly less than 40,000 of them were native Hawaiians. The queen faced serious difficulties in maintaining the legitimacy of Hawaiian political control as different groups organized themselves against her: the Patriotic League, which consisted of anti-royalists, and Lorrin Thurston's Annexation Club. No need to explain its purpose…and his club organized another group of thirteen men called the Committee of Safety, armed and threatening.

Lili'uokalani was not a weak queen. She had never been happy about the Bayonet Constitution. She was determined to replace it with one that restored the Hawaiian monarchy's powers, enabling her to properly care for and ensure the well-being of Hawaiians. But she didn't have an army to enforce her will, and she knew it. The last thing she was about to do was ask her people to lose their lives in a pointless battle that would end up with the loss of Hawai'i even if they fought bravely.

The queen was at home in Washington Place on August 12, 1898 on the day that the Republic of Hawai'i became the Territory of Hawai'i, no longer a rogue nation but a part of the United States. It had been just five years since it was the Kingdom of Hawai'i.

Queen Lili'oukalani

On that day, Queen Lili'uokalani sat in mourning in her living room, surrounded by her niece and nephews, the Princess Ka'iulani and the Princes David Kawananakoa and Kuhio. She had done her utmost to stop this from happening, traveling to Washington, D.C. with the anti-annexation petition and staying to attend social and diplomatic functions, all to no avail.

The family stayed at Washington Place, dressed in dark clothing, unsmiling, and heard the ceremony progressing just a block away at 'Iolani Palace. They heard the Royal Hawaiian Band, which had been forced to go by a different name, the Provisional Government Band, playing outside. The band was led by Henry Berger in a last rendition of King Kalakaua's *Hawai'i Pono'i,* and the old bandmaster cried. Then he raised his baton and led the band in playing Francis Scott Key's *The Star-Spangled Banner.* Everyone had just been given new citizenship with the stroke of a pen.

When it was over, the Hawaiian flag was taken down and the U.S. flag raised over Iolani Palace. Someone brought the Hawaiian flag, all folded up, over to Washington Place and gave it to the queen. I suppose that that was the best thing to do with it at that point, but she must have felt like a soldier's widow being given the flag that had been draped over her dead husband's coffin at the end of a funeral.

The Theft is Accomplished

The Big Five bullies knew what she was like, and made sure that her Cabinet would not support her. When the effort fell through, at least Queen Lili'uokalani knew that she had done her duty and tried, doomed to failure as it was. She surrendered in 1893, just 12 days short of two years on her throne, and was escorted from her palace.

American Minister John Stevens had assisted in the theft, despite the lack of express authority from the President to do so. He had provided the usurpers with American troops from U.S. Navy ships that were docked in Pearl Harbor. The queen, lacking even the semblance of an equal force, decided to live to fight another day.

By that time, President Cleveland, a Democrat, had sent an investigator by the name of James H. Blount to Hawai'i in 1893 to see what had happened. The president accepted Blount's analysis that the nation had been stolen. He refused to recommend that the U.S. Congress discuss annexing Hawai'i.

But it wasn't enough to restore the queen to her throne.

Her opponents from the United States, who did not live in Hawai'i but who wanted possession of it, sent someone else. He was Albert S. Willis, and he was officially there to apologize for the actions of Minister Stevens. Unofficially, he was to find out what the queen intended to do about the usurpers if she were to be reinstated. He came away from the meeting with a rather convenient misunderstanding, which was that she would have them beheaded. She had no such intention, but the damage was done.

The Republic of Hawai'i was established on July 4, 1894, with pineapple baron Sanford B. Dole installed as its President. The irony and hypocrisy of doing this on the date of Independence Day for the United States was not lost on the Hawaiians. Before long, a campaign to have Hawaii annexed as a territory to the United States was underway.

In 1895, the queen was formally deposed, despite her hopes that the United States would rescind the actions of the usurpers. When they deposed her, they presented the queen with a document saying that she ceded away her political powers. She asked them how they wanted her to sign it. "Lili'uokalani Dominis," came the reply.

The Theft is Accomplished

She looked at them, wondering whether or not they were serious; queens do not take their husbands' surnames, after all, so that was never her legal name. The signature would be a bogus one. She asked them if they were sure about that, and they said yes, caught up in the fun of humiliating her. She did it, not being inclined to enlighten them.

The Queen Fights Back
– With an Anti-Annexation Petition

But Liliʻuokalani wasn't going to just give up, and neither were her people.

There was a plan to restore the monarchy. One of its leaders was a man named Robert William Kalanikiapo Wilcox, who had received military training in Europe during Kalakaua's reign. He was Hawaiian on his mother's side, and aliʻi, too. But he was caught, along with the rest of the queen's supporters. She did not realize what was going on, because they had not told her about any of it.

The Big Five managed to uncover (or perhaps plant) some weapons in her gardens.

Wilcox and Prince Kuhio ended up in prison together. Kuhio's fiancée visited him and wrote to him daily. He was free after a year, which was the entire prison term. Wilcox got 3 years.

The usurpers arrested the queen and locked her in the palace for eight months, in an upstairs room, to be visited only by one of their wives during the day, and forbidden to walk on the lanai (veranda/balcony) outside her room until after dark. She sewed a quilt with nine sections during her captivity, deprived of most news but determined to record her plight in the decorative stitching on the quilt, plus her family tree.

At last she was allowed out, having been insulted during her imprisonment at the palace on the ludicrous charge of treason. She refused to break during her sham of a slanted trial, sitting stoically throughout the entire insulting experience.

The charge of treason was changed to "misprision of treason", which meant that she was accused of knowing all about the overthrow and doing nothing to stop it. What else was a deposed queen supposed to do?! She certainly wasn't going to act like the usurpers had any right to her realm. Fighting the situation was the honorable course of action, not behaving as if she had sworn allegiance to her usurpers.

They knew what they were; they told her that she was to be confined to Washington Place for five more months, then to the island

The Queen Fights Back

of Oʻahu for eight months after that, and then they gave her a passport and said she could travel. It was 1897.

Off she went, glad to feel free, with two loyal Hawaiians as traveling companions.

Her itinerary was not announced, as she didn't want to be prevented from going.

As she left, a rainbow was seen by her Hawaiian subjects, a sign that an aliʻi is traveling.

She was armed with a petition against the annexation of Hawaiʻi.

It had been signed by approximately 38,000 of the 40,000 native people of her stolen nation, with separate sections for men and women at the queen's instructions. Hawaiians don't discriminate against women as other cultures do, but Liliʻuokalani was taking no chances. She wanted something to present to the U.S. President and Congress that they couldn't dismiss.

She went to Washington, D.C., and attended many events so that influential people in government and society there could see that she was an educated, cultured head of state, not some barbarian. They saw it.

She went to Boston, Massachusetts to see her in-laws and friends. She and her husband had gone there together years before. They all welcomed her back with great affection, sympathy, and outrage over what had happened to her and to Hawaiʻi.

But they couldn't fix it.

The queen wrote and published her autobiography, telling not only the story of her life but also her side of the story of her country's loss, while in the United States, where Dole, Thurston, and the others could not get to her. It is both in print and available as an e-book: *Hawaiʻi's Story by Hawaiʻi's Queen*.

While in Boston, the queen made a doll to show how Hawaiian women looked and dressed at the time. She named it for her niece, Kaʻiulani. Princess Kaʻiulani heard about it while she was in England, waiting to be told that she could return home.

Annexed Anyway

The annexation happened anyway, in 1898.

President Cleveland had made only lame efforts to assist the Hawaiians, despite his gracious behavior toward the aliʻi. He did not sign off on the annexation, instead leaving it to the Republican administration of President William McKinley, which took office in 1897. Ignoring the petition against annexation, he and the U.S. Congress went ahead and annexed Hawaiʻi.

The temptation was too great to pass on having full ownership and control of Hawaiʻi so that, 1. The naval base at Pearl Harbor could be permanently at the disposal of the United States, and 2. The tropical paradise could be a territory of the United States. The Spanish-American War was underway, and the Americans wanted a conveniently located port in the Pacific Ocean. Hawaiʻi, less than but almost halfway across to the Philippines, was the ideal stopover.

There was a ceremony, and Queen Liliʻuokalani, her niece Princess Kaʻiulani, and other aliʻi were invited, but they all stayed away. Kaʻiulani had put on a brave face at social event after social event, attending them with haole thieves with a polite smile and never discussing the deteriorating political situation, but the idea of attending this event was too much. She spent the day with her aunt, quietly, mourning the loss of her country.

During the last few years of the nineteenth century, many native Hawaiian people visited the princess and the deposed queen, behaving as their tradition dictated, bringing small gifts such as chickens, or just coming to show that they were glad to still have an aliʻi nui to visit.

The princess and the queen could not fail to notice that most of them were living in poverty, with a standard far below that of the haoles who had stolen the Islands. The aliʻi could do very little about it at that point, as the thieves had abolished the posts of governor of each Island, something that the Hawaiians had maintained since the reign of Kamehameha the Great.

These were the same people who were able to boast of having the highest literacy rate on the planet, the result of Queen Kaʻahumanu's decision to require that every Hawaiian learn to read and write. They had lost their country...but they were ready and able to vote intelligently, keeping informed of political events.

Now all that the ali'i had left to offer their people were hospitals and schools that had been established using their own personal wealth for the exclusive benefit of native Hawaiian people. These institutions are still functioning today, and they have helped many Hawaiians, but there is also a significant number of homeless native Hawaiians. They are not easy to spot, because the state government of Hawai'i has done its best to force them out of the potential sight of tourists, who are a lucrative source of income and thus treated as more valuable than native Hawaiians.

Queen Lili'uokalani retired to Washington Place, occasionally spending time at her beach residence in Waikiki, and died at the age of 79 in 1917.

Not As the Big Five Planned It

The thieves had planned the theft of Hawai'i rather differently than the way it turned out. They had planned to require voters to own property, a thing that was alien to Hawaiian culture. But literacy became the requirement instead, and the Big Five had to accept the fact that Hawaiian men could vote. Not only that, but Prince Kuhio and Robert Wilcox each went to Washington, D.C., where they found places in the U.S. Congress to represent Hawaiian interests.

Prince Kawananakoa became active in politics as well, participating in a national presidential convention on Hawai'i's behalf. If they couldn't have an independent nation, these ali'i were determined to do whatever they could to look after Hawai'i's interests via other avenues.

This theft had not gone off without a hitch after all. The Big Five fumed. There was nothing they could do about it, other than to keep making money and abusing the press by intimidating the Hawaiian-language newspapers as much as they could for their opposing point of view about plantation management, labor relations, and promulgating other repressive policies.

The Big Five men had gotten away with the most insular of representation in all facets of Hawai'ian life as long as it was a territory of the United States, with a handful of the same men holding multiple board positions on education, labor, utilities, and transportation boards, and in governmental posts.

A U.S. Naval Base

The Merrie Monarch had a financially disastrous reign, so ten years after the theft of Hawai'i, the United States pushed for more: a naval base in Pearl Harbor for its exclusive use. King Kalakaua's foreign minister, Walter Murray Gibson, argued that this was impossible.

Undeterred, and taking advantage of the Hawaiian national debt, the U.S. Congress drew up a new reciprocity treaty in 1887 with the exclusive right to use Pearl Harbor attached in a separate convention (treaty).

Once it had that, the United States only had to wait until the time was ripe to annex all of Hawai'i. In 1900, with its naval base firmly entrenched after the 1898 Spanish-American War, the U.S. was free and clear to use the harbor as it wished.

The build-up took place gradually over the next forty years. The U.S. flag flew over Pearl Harbor, and naval technology moved in bit by bit. Shipyards and drydocks would be necessary to build and maintain the fleet. The first drydock was a failure; it collapsed in 1913 when it was almost finished. Religion was invoked – traditional Hawaiian religion – to prevent a repeat of this: a kahuna was invited to bless the next drydock project. That worked.

There were more military ships brought in year after year, though many were built elsewhere and moved to Pearl Harbor after the fact. As aviation became a part of the U.S. military machine, airstrips, fields, and hangars were built on the land surrounding the harbor and on Ford Island.

Submarines, amphibious airplanes, destroyers, battleships, tugboats, and other craft lined and littered Pearl Harbor. What was once a food source became completely militarized within the space of a century, transforming a millennium-long scene irrevocably.

To fuel all this, first coal and then oil was required. A series of oil tanks were thus installed on Hickam Field, on the southeast side of Pearl Harbor.

How the Big Five Ruined Hawai'i for Hawaiians

The Big Five built luxury hotels, starting with that huge, rambling pink one called the Royal Hawaiian Hotel in Waikiki, completed and opened in 1872, and have continued until there is nothing now but developed, heavily built-up land everywhere one looks in the area.

In 1921, they had an area in Waikiki, a wetlands that stretched back into Manoa and had been cultivated for crops by Hawaiians for centuries, filled in. Construction began on a canal, called the Ala Wai. Its purpose was to drain the wetlands and associated streams and then serve as a northern border for the Waikiki district, which became a tourist destination. It was finished in 1928. It is a fetid, unsanitary place that had untreated sewage dumped into it after severe storms in 2006. One person fell in, contracted cholera, and died.

Queen Lili'uokalani had a summer place in that area once.

The Hawaiian people had fed themselves there with their own labor, as their own bosses.

No more.

If they needed an income, there were always the plantations, said the Big Five barons. The plantations had overseers who wielded whips, spoke harshly to the workers, and paid a pittance. The Hawaiians had never lived like that, and they weren't about to start.

The Big Five imported more foreign labor; the precedent had already been set in the nineteenth century by inviting Chinese and Japanese laborers, who then sent for mail-order brides and stayed. Portuguese workers followed; they invented the ukulele.

Hawaiians, dispossessed, ended up in menial jobs, in Hell's Half Acre, a slum area of Honolulu, jammed into unsanitary, ramshackle tenements with few toilets or sinks, with shared kitchen facilities, to scratch out a living. The ali'i were still around, but for the most part only on call in a dire emergency. The princesses had money, but they couldn't solve everything.

The Racist Haole Woman Who Lied

These abuses did not change even when they were exposed by the Massie case in 1930-1932. A haole woman by the name of Thalia Massie, aged 19, a relative of Teddy Roosevelt by way of an illegitimate cousin, was living with her husband in the Manoa neighborhood of Honolulu while her husband, Tommie, was serving in the U.S. Navy.

Thalia was an unfaithful wife who loved to party. She suffered from undiagnosed and untreated Graves' Disease, which made her almost blind and gave her an odd gait. Tommie had a terrible temper, and in later years was diagnosed as a schizophrenic.

One night in the fall of 1930, Thalia, who hated living on the remote Islands, which would not be connected to the mainland of the United States by underwater communications cable until the next year, got into a fight with a boyfriend, and he hit her in the face.

Tommie had taken off earlier with other friends after insisting that she go out with him.

Walking back in the dark, Thalia got a ride from some passing American haoles, whom she could not see very well. She had leaned into their car window to ask if they were white, which had amazed them, as it was not that dim out.

When she and Tommie were both home, she concocted a rape story to explain her face.

He called the police. The Honolulu police consisted of both native Hawai'ian and white men – no women – and some others, including a man upon whose career the character Charlie Chan was based, Chang Apana. The highest-ranking officers were white.

A doctor and nurse at the local hospital examined her and found no evidence of rape.

Regardless, five men were chosen as likely suspects, trotted out in front of Thalia, who calmly put her glasses on, and accused them of being the perpetrators. They were Hawaiian, Chinese, Japanese, and various combinations of those ancestries. Their names were: Ben Ahakuelo, Henry Chang, Horace Ida, Joe Kahahawai, and David Takai.

The police proceeded to build a case against them, and the U.S. Navy was squarely behind it, with frequent and irate visits by the commanding admiral to the governor on behalf of the lying haole accuser.

The car that the men had used while out together the night before was found – it belonged to the sister of one of them – Horace Ida – and driven to the alleged crime scene. The officer heading the investigation deliberately made tracks there with its tires.

When the white officer who functioned as the C.S.I. investigator was asked to photograph the tracks, he packed up his camera and got back into the car to wait for the return ride to the police station. He refused to aid and abet in the fabrication of evidence.

A brilliant defense attorney represented one of the falsely accused men, a mixed white-Hawai'ian named William Heen. Heen was contacted after the mother of Ben Ahakuelo called Princess Abigail, the widow of Prince David Kawananakoa, desperate for help.

Princess Abigail was entertaining the visiting king and queen of Siam when that call came, but saw her first duty as being to her people if they needed her. She didn't go back to her guests until she had called William Heen and asked him to help. He told Abigail that he would meet the accused, and that if he thought the man was innocent, he would take his case.

Heen took the case. He ably defended the lot of them along with the other attorneys for the defense, while the prosecutor proceeded to dig himself into a hole of lies that he couldn't climb back out of.

The men were acquitted.

The Dishonor Killing

Thalia's self-entitled mother, Grace Fortescue, found this outcome unacceptable. She rounded up Tommie and two rough sailors to kidnap one of the falsely accused, Joe Kahahawai. They murdered him at her rented house, and attempted to drive to a cliff with a strong current swooshing into an underwater cavern to dispose of his body, but were caught.

Clarence Darrow, the hero of the Scopes Trial on evolution, broke due to the Crash of 1929, agreed to come out of retirement to defend the criminals. He tried the case as an honor killing, while the women of the Big Five put up posters everywhere they could find space that depicted Hawai'ian men as lecherous raping monsters peering out from behind palm leaves.

This, despite the fact that Hawaiian men had earned themselves just the opposite reputation by being respectful of women. They were good people living in a stolen land being judged and subjected to the cultural prejudices of the thieves.

No one bought any of the defense's claims, least of all the jury, which was a mix of white men and those of other resident races. No, the guilt of this group was obvious. It didn't matter that lynching was a common and widely accepted practice in the South on the mainland. It was murder, and this wasn't the South. Clarence Darrow annoyed the jurors by talking to them as if they were back-country ignoramuses, too.

The jurors who almost ruled for acquittal could not go through with it; the prosecution was being handled by a competent, experienced attorney, and this time the evidence – a dead body, a sheet from the house, blood, a weapon, and so on and on – backed up the charge.

The group was convicted of the crime, and a sentence was handed down: 10 years hard labor. But...Governor Judd was persuaded to commute it to time served aboard the navy ship that had housed Mrs. Fortescue during the investigation and trial, plus one hour in his office for the lot of them. Grinning smugly for the press, the group posed outside the capitol building for photographs.

Governor Judd later hired the Pinkerton National Detective Agency of New York City to investigate the entire matter, which was paid for by the Territory of Hawai'i. The agency's conclusion, which he kept private, was that no rape had ever occurred – only rampant racism – but that a horrible murder had. Judd kept the finding quiet because the uproar over it had only just died down; no one in government there wanted to revisit it.

Things went back to the way they had been.

Battleship Row with the USS *Arizona*

The USS *Arizona* was ahead of its time in that it was fueled by gasoline, not coal. It was constructed in the New York Navy Yard in 1916, but never saw any action in World War I. Its entire role in that conflict was to bring home as many surviving soldiers as it could carry.

The *Arizona* was upgraded in the 1920s with more advanced weapons as technology continued to advance, and then again in 1935 to increase its crew capacity from 1,000 to 1,700. In between upgrades, in 1931, the ship was sent to the Pacific via the Panama Canal, to San Diego, California. By 1941, the *Arizona* had spent a year based in Pearl Harbor after another transfer.

The *Arizona* was one of the most heavily-armed ships in the fleet. It had plenty of company in Pearl Harbor. It was moored among several others in a lineup called Battleship Row. The white-painted, hexagonal quays of Battleship Row are still in place, even though they are now longer in use. Just look on Google Maps or Google Earth, and zoom in on Pearl Harbor to see it for yourself.

This is the quay for the USS *Arizona*, which was named BB-39 before it got its name.

All this preparation and armament was no longer about any threat from any European power with colonies in the South Pacific. It was about Japan. Japan was busy building itself an empire in that region. Poor in natural resources, Japan was spending the decades after World War I building up its military forces and annexing whatever territory it could conquer.

Emperor Hirohito came to the Chrysanthemum Throne in 1926. Although he was fascinated by zoology and marine biology, he also wanted an empire to justify his title. Japan had been forced by U.S. Commodore Matthew Perry to open itself to foreign trade in 1854, and it viewed that as a humiliation that needed avenging. It also wanted a military force as large and as strong as those of the U.S. and European nations.

His generals were happy to oblige; among them were Japanese Imperial Army General Hideki Tojo, who went on to become prime minister, Japanese Imperial Navy Admiral Isoroku Yamamoto, who commanded his nation's navy, and Vice Admiral Chuichi Nagumo, who commanded Japan's First Air Fleet.

Tojo was hanged after World War II. Yamamoto's plane was shot down in April of 1943. Nagumo committed suicide – by shooting himself in the head rather than by hara-kiri/seppuku – in July of 1944 when it became clear that Japan would lose the war.

World War II Deposes the Big Five

When the Japanese attacked Pearl Harbor, things changed.

The U.S. Navy militarized the Islands, seizing all resources and governmental control, instituting martial law, and breaking the Big Five's stranglehold. The Matson shipping company felt the change keenly when their luxury ocean liners, which had made supply and passenger runs between the Islands and San Francisco, Los Angeles, Oregon, and Washington, were seized and painted gray.

Blackout rules applied to all windows and street lights in case the Japanese decided to come back…even though they preferred to attack on weekends, holidays, and daylight. Of course, the Navy couldn't know that they weren't coming back.

Supplies ran low, and goods often rotted on the docks as the Navy considered the Big Five exports to be a low priority next to the war effort.

Hawaiian residents of Japanese descent watched as their sons demanded a role in the war effort, offering to go fight and die in the European theater, where their presence would not raise concerns of loyalty to Emperor Hirohito's expanding empire. They served with distinction, winning medals, and some came home to a hero's welcome. At last, Japanese residents were established as citizens rather than foreigners on the Islands.

A Disparity of Resources

On the United States end of the conflict, resources were split between a suspiciously calm Pacific scene and an openly hostile Atlantic that had been on full alert since 1939, when Hitler had invaded Poland, kicking off World War II.

That was the problem.

In 1940, one-third of everything that the U.S. Navy had in the Pacific had been transferred to the Atlantic to counterbalance Nazi Germany's resources. This left the U.S. exposed on its left flank, and the admirals in charge at Pearl Harbor knew it.

Nonetheless, they were in charge, so they got blamed for what followed.

They had been warned that any attack from the Japanese would come on a U.S. holiday or a weekend, just when Americans were relaxing and not focused on defense or work. Even so, without sufficient resources to mount a comparable defense, heavy damage from an attack would be the logical outcome.

Japan had 10 aircraft carriers in the Pacific, which was the latest and greatest technology of the time, making the battleship (and the *Arizona* was a battleship) only a support system. Still, battleships presented a credible and significant threat. The United States Navy had a grand total of 3 aircraft carriers in the Pacific, the *Saratoga*, the *Lexington*, and the *Enterprise*.

The scores only got worse for the U.S. from there. Battleships: Japan 12, U.S. 9. Cruisers: Japan 35, U.S. 21. Destroyers: Japan 110, U.S. 53.

It was only logical that the Japanese struck while the numbers remained thus.

Tora! Tora! But No Third Tora

So what were the Japanese planning?

Plenty: 3 air strikes, or waves, on Pearl Harbor with 5 miniature, 2-man submarines to sneak into the shallow waters of the harbor and add to the chaos with torpedoes. They planned to blow up: Battleship Row, to take out as many U.S. Navy ships as they could; Wheeler Field, a U.S. Army Air Force base; Bellows Field, its auxiliary base; Hickam Air Field, where the bomber planes were kept; 'Ewa Marine Air Station, which had 47 fighter planes; Kane'ohe Naval Air Station, in order wipe out the long-range reconnaissance fleet; and the oil tanks, so that resupplying after the attack would take as long as possible.

The planes were to fly south to Pearl Harbor from the aircraft carriers that had brought them via a circuitous route from Japan. It was not a suicide mission, even though many of the pilots rightly expected not to make it back to their ships. Still, if they could get back, that was the plan.

That seemed like a well-thought-out plan, but when plans are carried out, things go wrong.

At first, all was conducted in perfect secrecy, with the pilots told nothing until the 6 aircraft carriers, were well underway. Sake was served, and the first wave of pilots took off from the *Akagi*. Tora means "tiger" in Japanese, and although it was said three times, only two waves were ultimately sent out. Nagumo changed his mind about the third one, worried that he had lost the element of surprise.

That was a mistake – he could have destroyed the oil tanks and crippled the U.S. Navy.

The mini-subs weren't very effective either. One of them ended up beached on a reef by Kane'ohe. A key navigation instrument had been damaged, so the crew got lost. One died, and the other got captured and spent the duration of the war imprisoned on Sand Island. All 8 of the other submariners died. The 9 dead were honored for dying in the attack.

The Japanese considered capture to be a disgrace, so the tenth man wasn't mentioned. He asked permission to commit suicide in prison, which of course the Americans denied. It was the perfect culture clash;

the enemy considered suicide an honor, while the captors considered it a cop-out. That man was forced to live, and he eventually became a pacifist.

Another thing that went wrong for the Japanese was that the U.S. aircraft carriers were out on training exercises north of the Islands, so taking them out of the military equation wasn't an option. That was sheer luck on the part of the U.S. Navy.

Finally, one Japanese pilot got lost in the confusion after inflicting damage at Pearl Harbor and, with six bullet holes in his plane, headed west and crash-landed on the island of Ni'ihau.

Still, the damage done on O'ahu was considerable.

The planes on the ground were almost all destroyed, and the few that managed to take to the air in time to shoot back found little satisfaction to be had. They did have the consolation of knowing that they kept the attackers distracted from shooting at the oil tanks, at least.

The *Arizona* sank up to its upper deck in flames, with only its guns and turrets exposed. The captain of the *Nevada* tried to head out of the harbor, but once he realized that his ship was too badly damaged to make it, he deliberately ran it aground to prevent it from sinking and blocking the harbor entrance. It was later salvaged and restored to service. Other ships in Battleship Row that were hit were the *Oklahoma*, the *Maryland*, the *Tennessee*, and the *West Virginia*.

Three ships in drydock, the *Cassin*, *Downes*, and *Pennsylvania*, were set on fire. The minelayer *Oglala* and the destroyer *Shaw* were nearby, and they were struck too, as was a repair ship, the *Vestal*. Three cruisers were also hit: the *Raleigh*, the *Helena*, and the *Honolulu*.

On the far side of Ford Island by the Middle Loch, the *Curtiss* was torpedoed, but it was restored to service in 1942. The nearby *Utah* was also hit. South of Battleship Row, on the other side of Ford Island, was the *California*, in flames as well.

18 ships wrecked.

The Japanese had enjoyed a bit of luck in that the men watching the radar display at the Opana station in northern O'ahu had been told to ignore the blips that they saw. The radar blips were dismissed as a group of planes that were expected to come in from California, which gave the first wave of attackers that much longer to inflict a surprise attack.

40 civilians died from stray bullets fired from above. People came out of their homes and shops to look up – Hawaiians, Japanese-Americans, Chinese-Americans, Caucasians, and others. A significant number of the civilian dead included Japanese-Americans, and of those who lived, they remembered seeing the large red dots on the rudders of the Japanese planes and thinking of the rising sun symbol as an enemy attack, and most unwelcome.

The Niʻihau Incident

Shigenori Nishikaichi was part of the second wave of the attack on Pearl Harbor.

He had spent his entire life preparing for his role.

Now, flying west with six bullet strikes, including one to his fuel tank, he knew he could not get back to the *Hiryu*, the aircraft carrier that he had taken off from. It soon became clear to the pilot that he would have to crash-land on Niʻihau, known as the Forbidden Island.

Niʻihau is 124 miles away from Oʻahu, and is shaped sort of like a seal leaping up, facing northeast to Kauaʻi. It is entirely inhabited by native Hawaiians, owned by the Robinson family who live on Kauaʻi, and in 1941, 53-year-old Alymer Robinson was in charge.

Aylmer visited his property and checked on his wards, as he thought of the Niihauans, once a week. He got there by boat, always landing at Kii, which was the closest point from where he lived in Makaweli. He never married, and had plenty of time to concern himself with his business and the Niihauans. He kept the people under quarantine to protect them from pathogens that would compromise their immune system. The government let him do as he saw fit.

Life on the Forbidden Island was primitive, with wells, no electricity, and a dry, sunny climate. Education was provided by Aylmer through the fourth grade. After leaving school, the people tended to forget English and lapse exclusively into their own dialect of Hawaiian. They had honey, turkeys, ducks and other birds, cats and pigs that had gone feral, sheep, and horses. The men wore jeans and white shirts, and wore hunting knives in their belts. The women wore plain dresses in light colors. Firearms were banned.

Aylmer employed a Japanese couple, Yoshio and Irene Harada, as beekeepers on Niihau. They had moved there in 1938. In late 1941, Aylmer had appointed Yoshio to be paymaster also, after the previous one had died. He was to begin this duty in the new year. They lived in a house that Aylmer had provided. It had a radio, but that was for listening to the news, not for communicating with anyone else.

Yoshio's parents had been plantation workers on Kauai after immigrating from Japan. They had lived in segregation from the white

The Niʻihau Incident

plantation owners, and endured a degrading system of apartheid, into which their son was born.

Yoshio's parents returned to Japan before he was married, and although he never set foot there himself, he had grown up in a society that treated him as second-class and separate from the group that enjoyed full rights and privileges in American society.

Irene had traveled in Japan as an adult with her mother, and then returned to Hawaiʻi, where she met and married Yoshio. She considered her life on Niʻihau to be a horrible banishment. If she needed to communicate with Aylmer, he had told her to signal with torches, and a boat would come. There was no quick and convenient way to leave independently, and by design.

Another Japanese person lived on Niihau, an elderly man who had married a Niihauan woman. His name was Ishimatsu Shintani, and like the Haradas, he was denied the chance at having American citizenship. His wife had lost her own citizenship when she married him.

The Japanese pilot was about to land on an island that was ripe for trouble.

But there was a bit of good luck: 29-year-old Howard Kaleohano lived on Niʻihau. He was fluent in both written and spoken English, having been born and raised on the Big Island of Hawaiʻi, in Kona. He had come to Niʻihau as an adult and married a Niihauan woman, Mabel Kahale, and became a cowboy. There are cowboys on the Big Island, called paniolos, so perhaps he had learned his trade before moving away. He lived near the Haradas, in Kiekie, on the western side of Niʻihau, halfway down the coast.

Howard Kaleohano was the first person to encounter Nishikaichi when he stumbled out of his damaged plane, dazed and disoriented. Howard was well informed of the strained diplomatic relations between Japan and the United States to know that the presence of a Japanese fighter pilot on his island could not be a good omen.

The first thing Kaleohano did was to relieve Nishikaichi of his weapon, map, and papers.

The papers included the battle plans that the pilot had been carrying out.

Hawai'i – Stolen Paradise

After that, Kaleohano struck up a friendly conversation with the pilot while he decided on his next move. The pilot asked him if he was Japanese, which was not that odd considering the fact that the two men were of similar build, height and weight, but Kaleohano said no, he was Hawaiian. He led his "guest" toward the Robinson guest house.

Nishikaichi had difficulty communicating in English, and after asking for his papers back, he tried again on paper, but Kaleohano would not give them back. The pilot had a problem: he had to destroy his papers and plane completely so that the enemy would not be able to study them, or he would suffer permanent dishonor. It wasn't enough that he had seen that the attack had inflicted tremendous damage on Pearl Harbor.

Soon Kaleohano decided that he needed an interpreter, and curious neighbors were crowding around the house. He asked one of them to go and get Shintani, went outside to look at the downed plane, and saw the bullet holes.

Shintani arrived, spoke briefly with the pilot, turned pale, and left. He was too upset to explain what was going on, so the Haradas were sought next.

Yoshio came over, spoke with the pilot, found out all about the attack on Pearl Harbor this way, and decided not to tell the Niihauans about it just yet.

The Niihauans put on a luau for the pilot, played the ukulele, danced and sang, and fed him. They handed the instrument to the pilot, who played it like a Japanese samisen and sang them a song…while staying alert for any indication of a rescue submarine. It did not appear.

Then the Niihauans found out about the attack via a radio announcement; there were Hawaiian-language newspapers and radio stations on the Islands. The announcement ordered all civilians to black out their windows at night.

They confronted the pilot, and Harada translated it all this time.

The pilot was installed as the Haradas guest, with five guards, including Ben Kanahele.

The Niʻihau Incident

Meanwhile, Aylmer was concerned about being cut off from his wards, but he did not yet know what was going on.

As for the Niihauans, it was time for Aylmer to make his weekly visit, so they went to Kii and waited for him to appear. He did not. All inter-island travel had been stopped when the U.S. Navy declared martial law for the Islands.

The pilot worked on the Haradas, talking to them about Japan and their parents, who had retired to Japan, until they agreed to help him. Soon the game was afoot as Shintani visited Howard and asked for the papers, which yielded nothing. Howard Kaleohano was no fool.

But the Haradas managed to find and acquire the pilot's weapon, Yoshio fired it at Howard as he came out of his outhouse. Howard ran, and warned the Niihauans to evacuate the village and hide. The villagers heeded this and fled.

Howard was busy meanwhile. He hid the pilot's gun in his house and the papers in his mother-in-law's home. Then he took off with a group 5 of Niihauans for Kii. On the way, they set a bonfire at Paniau at 9 p.m., south of the landing point at Kii, hoping that Aylmer might see it. He did, and was very worried, but the Navy patrols would not allow him to go to Niʻihau.

Howard and his companions had to row for hours, with only a gallon of water and no food in the boat. The trip took 10 hours, from half past midnight to 10:30 a.m. the next morning. Howard called Aylmer from the Waimea police station and told him what was going on.

Aylmer met them, took them to a Chinese restaurant, and bought them a meal.

Now it was up to the U.S. Army officers on Kauaʻi to go to Niʻihau and rescue the residents.

Not all of the Japanese people who lived in Hawaiʻi had been raised as Yoshio Harada had. One of them was an army officer, 1st Lieutenant Jack Mizuha. He had been educated in the public schools of Kauai, raised in a home with a former Japanese samurai for a father, and viewed his cultural background as a part of his identity rather than a defining element of it.

Hawai'i – Stolen Paradise

Mizuha had learned Japanese in school, but knew English as a first language, and considered himself to be an American. He had been in command of the Burns Field until the attack on Pearl Harbor, after which anti-Japanese prejudice and paranoia caused him to be demoted.

Instead of taking offense and wanting to avenge the insult, Mizuha looked for an opportunity to prove himself to be a loyal American. As a Japanese descendant who had been born on the Islands, a Nikkei, he had U.S. citizenship, and now he intended to prove that he valued it.

Here was his chance. He called his new commander, Lieutenant Colonel Eugene J. Fitzgerald, and volunteered to lead a rescue mission on Niihau. Fitzgerald accepted. Another Nikkei, Ben Kobayashi, who was fluent in Japanese, offered his services as both a member of the team and translator. Mizuha accepted, and added him to the team.

Back on Niihau, the pilot and Harada had gone back to the plane and taken the machines guns out of it.

Harada and the pilot had grabbed two Niihauan men, Niau and Kalima, and tied their hands behind their backs once they were armed. Harada had fired at some Niihauans, so he was getting in deeper and deeper, feeling that there was no way out. The pilot kept checking the radio in his downed plane, and he and Harada got a wagon for the machine guns while Harada told the Niihauans that there was enough ammunition to kill everyone on the island.

But things weren't going well. There was no information about the Japanese fleet on the pilot's radio. They sent Kalima to tell Irene that Yoshio wasn't coming back yet. Kalima walked that way until he was out of sight, then took off. He found his wife, Ella, who untied him, then met up with Ben Kanahele and told him what was happening. The group of five Niihauans wandered in the darkness, while their armed enemies did the same nearby, looking for food.

The pilot and Harada had set Howard's house on fire, which Howard had seen from the rowboat, but bravely rowed onward. Next, they went into Howard's mother-in-law's house and found her there, lame and reading. She stared them down and they left without finding the papers and map, which Howard had hidden in there.

The invader and the traitor were also getting hungry, as were the Niihauans. When they each sneaked into the village to get some food, they ran into each other, and soon Ben Kanahele and his companions were captives...again.

They told Ben to go find Howard Kaleohano, and let him walk away. Ben knew where Howard was, but played along, calling him. Ben spoke in Hawaiian to his friends, telling them that they had to get that pistol away from the pilot and Harada before anyone got shot.

Everyone was looking quite tired and worn out from the stress of it all, and Harada was unbuttoning his shirt with hara-kiri rather obviously on his mind.

Ben and Ella pounced on the gun.

Harada pulled Ella away, and the pilot fired, wounding Ben in the chest, groin, and left hip.

Ella grabbed a rock and bashed Nishikaichi over the head with it. Ben turned around and grabbed the pilot as he did one of his sheep, by the neck, pulled his knife out of his belt, and slit his throat.

Harada loaded the gun again and shot himself twice.

It was over.

Mizuha didn't know that, however, and led his rescue team over the island until they all met up. Ella grabbed the guns and ran for help, but dropped them in the dark. (They were found five years later, after a rainstorm. Ben recovered from his wounds.) At last, Mizuha and his team, guided by Howard Kaleohano with Aylmer Robinson bringing up the rear, arrived.

Mabel Kaleohano came running to meet her husband, telling him that their house had been burned down. He hugged her and said he didn't care; what mattered was that they were okay.

Mizuha spent a week compiling data for his report, which he prepared in the schoolhouse.

Irene Harada was promptly carted off to Sand Island for the duration of the war. She was allowed out after that, reunited with her two daughters and son, and lived quietly on Kauaʻi until she died in 1996 at the age of 91. She was bitter about her experience on Niʻihau, like an angry child who had chosen the wrong side and blamed the winners for the outcome. Aylmer had no use for her after the incident on Niʻihau.

Her attitude and role in it was revealed when she granted interviews in Japanese, operating on the mistaken attitude that no one would translate and thus no English speaker would find out. That this was done was something that she considered to be a personal and cultural affront.

Ben Kahalele and Howard Kaleohano were each awarded the Medal of Freedom for their efforts, the highest honor that a U.S. civilian can receive. Ella Kahalele got no medal for her bravery and the physical risk she took, which was most likely due to sexism.

Jack Mizuha went on to fight in the 100th Infantry Battalion in the U.S. Army until he was wounded in the neck, after which he graduated from the University of Michigan Law School. From there had had a distinguished legal career in Hawaiʻi. He was appointed Attorney General when Hawaiʻi was still a territory in 1958, and again a year later when it became a state. After that, in 1961, Mizuha was appointed to be an Associate Justice of Hawaiʻi's Supreme Court.

U.S. Concentration Camps

It was because of the Niihau Incident, as it came to be known, that the U.S. government disgraced itself by dispossessing as many Japanese residents that it could find on the west coast of the mainland.

It took away their homes, businesses, jobs, chances at an education, and contact with all that had become theirs and familiar to them, and interred them in concentration camps without the comforts and amenities that other Americans enjoyed – heat, warm running water, and independence.

These camps were in a cold, barren desert area of the United States.

This was not done to Americans of Italian or German descent, despite the fact that the U.S. was at war with those nations as well as Japan. No...Italian-Americans and German-Americans were treated as loyal Americans.

In 1988, President Reagan apologized on behalf of the United States government, but it felt like too little, too late to the Americans whose lives were stolen from them for three years. After that, the U.S. government disbursed over $1.6 billion in reparations to those who had been interned in those camps, and to their heirs.

Japanese-American residents of Hawaii responded to the attacks by demanding an opportunity to fight in World War II...in Europe. This group of Nikkei made up the majority of the 100th Infantry Battalion. Many of them died, and they were awarded medals such as the Medal of Honor and the Purple Heart. Those who survived also served admirably.

When they came home as veterans of World War II, they were rightfully greeted as Americans.

Cleanup and War

Cleanup at Pearl Harbor began before the attack was over, with rescue attempts.

Plenty of movies have been made about the attack, both documenting and dramatizing it. The movies describe and explain every detail of the human costs as well as the financial and military ones. I have not watched each and every one of them, and I doubt that I will. Watching the same upsetting disaster over and over again and seeing sailors drown or get burned or die however they are shown dying repeatedly seems like a desensitizing pastime for someone who wasn't there. One movie has been enough for me thus far: *Pearl Harbor* of 2001, starring Ben Affleck, Josh Hartnett, and Kate Beckinsale.

When I returned from this trip to Hawai'i and showed my research materials to my cousin, an artist who makes very convincing skin-like veneers to cover titanium prosthetics (arms and legs mostly) for war veterans and other amputees, he talked about those movies. One thing that stayed in his memory was a scene of the sailors below decks as the *Arizona* was sinking. A large, strong sailor opened a porthole and pushed his buddies out as fast as he could, then tried to follow, only to realize that he was too big and too muscular to fit through the hole. He was trapped.

Until I visited the memorial, I had guessed that the men who died on that ship had drowned, suffering terrible pain their lungs as they filled up with water, and at last blacking out.

That wasn't what happened, the National Parks Ranger told us. They burned to death.

There are no skeletons in the *Arizona*, only ashes that have washed away into the harbor.

After the attack, the U.S. Congress was suddenly amenable to funding the Pacific fleet.

All of Hawai'i became militarized, and cinemas all over the nation showed newsreels before the main features that stirred up American resolve to put as much energy and resources as they could manage into the war effort. Martial law took over the entire Territory of Hawai'i,

Cleanup and War

including the courts, the shipping industry, and the police. Nothing got in or out – not goods, not information, not anything – without permission from the U.S. military.

Everything that was above the water level on the *Arizona* was removed and salvaged, while everything below was left as a memorial tomb for the sailors. The upper deck is just below the water level, so it can easily be seen from above. Plumes of gasoline still bubble up from the hull. This view can be seen on the Internet without traveling to Pearl Harbor; just go to Google Maps or Google Earth, click the Satellite View option, and look. One can do a lot of armchair travel this way.

The attack on Pearl Harbor was ultimately avenged in a direct way when the U.S. Army Air Force sank all of the Japanese aircraft carriers that had brought the planes on December 7, 1941.

The plane that Shigenori Nishikaichi flew and crash-landed on Niʻihau has been moved to the Pacific Aviation Museum on Ford Island. It can be reached via the bridge that crosses the East Loch. So much for his plan to destroy his plane, map, and papers.

Fires on board the damaged ships were put out. It took two days for the *Arizona* to stop burning. The *California*, the *West Virginia*, the *Pennsylvania*, the *Tennessee*, and the *Nevada* were salvageable. The *Shaw*, *Cassin*, and *Helm* were also repaired and returned to service. The *Oklahoma* was capsized and declared a total loss. So was the *Utah*.

Divers went underwater to see what could be salvaged. Women trained in the use of fire hoses in case of another attack. They also participated alongside men in salvage efforts above the water. This work took two years. By 1943, Pearl Harbor looked almost normal and was fully functional again, except for the sunken wreckage of the *Arizona*.

The U.S. certainly paid back Japan for Pearl Harbor many, many times over when it dropped atomic bombs on the civilian cities of Hiroshima and Nagasaki in August of 1945. Those weapons killed so many people that Emperor Hirohito went on the radio and told his people to stop fighting. They had never heard his voice before. The U.S. government had become convinced that nothing else would motivate the Japanese to stop fighting.

Hawai'i – Stolen Paradise

Surrender documents were signed aboard the USS *Missouri* on September 2, 1945. The ship was moored in Tokyo Bay for that, and a Who's Who List of Allied military commanders were in attendance, with representatives from not only the United States but also Britain, China, Australia, New Zealand, Canada, France, and the Netherlands. General Douglas MacArthur and Fleet Admiral Chester Nimitz watched as Japanese Foreign Minister Mamoru Shigemitsu signed on the required line.

The same 31-star American flag that Commodore Matthew Perry had flown on his ship in 1854 when he forced Japan to open its doors to Western trade was flown on the *Missouri*, most likely to rub the Japanese noses in their second defeat.

That was it. No tea, no nothing. Good-bye and get off our ship, Shigemitsu.

Peace and Creating a Memorial

The *Missouri* returned to service and saw duty in the Korean War, then it sat in the Pacific for 29 years until it was updated and upgraded in 1984. It saw duty in the Kuwait War, and then was decommissioned in 1992 due to budget cuts. In 1998, it became a museum ship, and has been moored close to the USS *Arizona* Memorial since that time.

After World War II, nothing more happened with the USS *Arizona* until 1950, when Admiral Arthur Radford, the Commander of the Pacific Fleet, ordered that a small platform be attached to its hull so that a flag could be flown over the wreckage.

But that wasn't good enough. In 1958, The U.S. Congress authorized funds for a better and more permanent memorial over the sunken ship. Even that wasn't enough money, however. In 1961, Elvis Presley put on a concert and donated every cent earned from it to the project.

The memorial was designed by Alfred Preis. It is 182 feet long, all in white, and it tapers in the middle, curving inwards from above and on its sides, with seven openings above showing the sky, plus seven more on either side. There is no glass; one can look straight up and out of them.

It opened on Memorial Day in 1962. A U.S. flag flies above it.

The USS *Arizona* Memorial today, with the American flag flying over it.

The Visitor Center grounds include the anchor of the USS *Arizona*, which has been raised, painted gray, and placed directly across the East Loch from the sunken wreckage.

Hawai'i – Stolen Paradise

The anchor of the USS *Arizona*.

Hawai'i Becomes Five-O in 1959

The Hawaiian Islands became the 50th state on August 21, 1959.

That's why the television show about cops in Honolulu is called *Hawaii Five-O* – it signifies that Hawai'i is the 50th state in the Union. The show gives the impression that the police station is in Ali'iolani Hale, the legislative palace across the street from 'Iolani Palace. Alex O'Loughlin's character, Commander McGarrett, went into the Ala Wai Canal in a recent episode, and all I could think of was that he would get a lethal plague. Instead, he dragged out the suspect, and then injected himself with a vaccine once he was back at the police station.

In November of 1993, President Clinton apologized formally to the Hawaiian people for the theft of their country, by signing a document issued by the U.S. Congress. There are Hawaiians who would like their nation's sovereignty returned, and their lands back, but they lack the numbers and political clout to achieve that. The U.S. Supreme Court has been unhelpful, siding with the State of Hawaii in a 1999 case, construing that apology as strictly symbolic.

Today, Hawai'i has universities, with some native people on their boards and faculties, and not all of them are ali'i. It also has hospitals, museums, and lush gardens, some set up by foreigners who moved in, and some by ali'i. There are few speakers of the Hawaiian language, but hula dance is in full swing all over the Island along with Hawaiian music. It's about more than merely providing a pleasant atmosphere for tourists. One can major in hula dance in Hawaiian college programs. There are even Hawaiian history and culture courses at other universities in other states, including, I found out at home, in Connecticut.

The Hawaiians lost their country for many reasons, but one of them is that their Islands are so beautiful in every way: beautiful for the flora and fauna, beautiful for the music and dance, and beautiful most of all for the friendliness of the people themselves.

For that, haoles want to visit them and their Islands again and again.

Bibliography

Some of these sources were printed copies, but most were e-books downloaded to a Nook Color device. Many of the items from the 19th and early 20th centuries were scanned as they were into a computer, skewing the images somewhat. Other texts included Hawaiian language punctuation and character markings that came through on the electronic reader as boxes, which made it difficult to learn the words as they should appear.

Humor

1. Mark Twain/Samuel Langhorne Clemens. MARK TWAIN IN HAWAI'I: ROUGHING IT IN THE SANDWICH ISLANDS – HAWAI'I IN THE 1860S. Foreword by A. Grove Day. Honolulu, Hawai'i: Mutual Publishing. 1990.

Fiction

2. Jack London. THE HOUSE OF PRIDE. Barnes & Noble edition published by B&R Samizdat Express. 1912.

3. Robert Louis Stevenson. THE BOTTLE IMP. Barnes & Noble edition published by B & R Samizdat Express. 1891.

4. Alan Brennert. HONOLULU. New York, New York: St. Martin's Griffin. 2009.

5. Michael Crichton and Richard Preston. MICRO. New York, New York: Harper. 2011.

Poetry

6. John Dominis Holt. HANAI: A POEM FOR QUEEN LILI'UOKALANI. Honolulu, Hawai'i: Hawai'i: Topgallant Publishing Co., Ltd. 1986.

Music

Bibliography

7. King David Kalakaua, Queen Lili'uokalani, Princess Likelike, and Prince Leleiohoku II. NA LANI 'EHA. Selected songs written by the four royal siblings featuring Ku'uipo Kumukahi and The Hawai'ian Music Hall of Fame Serenaders. Honolulu, Hawai'i: The Hawaiian Music Hall of Fame. 2007.

8. Scott C.S. Stone and bandmaster Aaron David Mahi. THE ROYAL HAWAIIAN BAND: ITS LEGACY. CD Recording: Leon Siu, Producer – Haku Mele Hawai'i; Dale P. Madden – Island Heritage. Honolulu, Hawai'i: Island Heritage Publishing. 2004.

Autobiographical, Biographical, Social, Political, and Cultural History

9. Manley Hopkins. HAWAI'I: THE PAST, PRESENT, AND FUTURE OF ITS ISLAND-KINGDOM. AN HISTORICAL ACCOUNT OF THE SANDWICH ISLANDS (POLYNESIA). London, England: Longmans, Green, and Co. 1866.

10. Lydia Liliu Loloku Walania Wewehi Kamakaeha Lili'uokalani. HAWAI'I'S STORY BY HAWAI'I'S QUEEN [Illustrated]. Boston, Massachusetts: Lothrop, Lee & Shepard. 1897.

11. Professor William De Witt Alexander. HISTORY OF LATER YEARS OF THE HAWAI'IAN MONARCHY...AND THE REVOLUTION OF 1893. Hawai'ian Copyright by W. D. Alexander. October 16th, 1897.

12. David Malo, translated by Nathaniel B. Emerson. HAWAIIAN ANTIQUITIES, MO'OLELO HAWAI'I. Honolulu, Hawai'i: Bernice Pauahi Bishop Museum. 1898.

13. Elizabeth Kekaaniauokalani Kalaninuiohilaukapu Pratt, Great-great-granddaughter of Keoua. HISTORY OF KEOWA KALANIKUPUAPA-I-KALANI-NUI, FATHER OF HAWAI'I KINGS, AND HIS DESCENDANTS, WITH NOTES ON KAMEHAMEHA I, FIRST KING OF ALL HAWAI'I. Honolulu, Territory of Hawai'i. 1920.

14. Alexander MacDonald. REVOLT IN PARADISE – THE SOCIAL REVOLUTION IN HAWAI'I AFTER PEARL HARBOR. New York, N.Y.: Steven Daye, Inc. 1944.

15. Richard A. Wisniewski. THE RISE AND FALL OF THE HAWAI'IAN KINGDOM: A PICTORIAL HISTORY. Honolulu, Hawai'i: Pacific Basin Enterprises. 1979.

16. Allan Beekman. THE NI'IHAU INCIDENT. *The true story of the Japanese fighter pilot who, after the Pearl Harbor attack, crash-landed on the Hawai'ian Island of Ni'ihau and terrorized the residents.* Honolulu, Hawai'i: Heritage Press of Pacific. 1982.

17. Richard Zeigler and Patrick M. Patterson. RED SUN: THE INVASION OF HAWAI'I AFTER PEARL HARBOR – A FICTIONAL HISTORY. Honolulu, Hawai'i: The Bess Press. 2001.

18. Noenoe K. Silva. ALOHA BETRAYED: NATIVE HAWAI'IAN RESISTANCE TO AMERICAN COLONIALISM. Durham, South Carolina & London, England: Duke University Press. 2004.

19. Scott C.S. Stone, photographs by Mazeppa King Costa. THE ROYAL HAWAIIAN BAND: ITS LEGACY. Honolulu, Hawai'i: Island Heritage Publishing. 2004.

20. David Stannard. HONOR KILLING: RACE, RAPE, AND CLARENCE DARROW'S SPECTACULAR LAST CASE. New York, N.Y.: Penguin Books. 2005.

21. Allan Seiden. THE HAWAI'IAN MONARCHY. Honolulu, Hawai'i: Mutual Publishing. 2005.

22. Alton Pryor. LITTLE KNOWN TALES IN HAWAI'IAN HISTORY. Roseville, California: Stagecoach Publishing at Smashwords. 2011.

23. Nancy Webb and Jean Francis Webb. KA'IULANI: CROWN PRINCESS OF HAWAI'I. 4th Edition. Honolulu, Hawai'i: Mutual Publishing. 2011.

24. Allan Seiden. PEARL HARBOR – FROM FISHPONDS TO WARSHIPS: A COMPLETE ILLUSTRATED HISTORY. 18th printing, softcover. Honolulu, Hawai'i: Mutual Publishing. 2012.

News Articles

Bibliography

25. Associated Press and United Press. "War! Oahu Bombed by Japanese Planes – Six Known Dead, 21 Injured, at Emergency Hospital." *Honolulu Star-Bulletin 1st Extra*. Sunday, December 7, 1941. Evening Bulletin, Est. 1882, No. 11287. Hawaiian Star, Vol. XLVIII' No. 15359.

26. "Movement for Sovereignty is Growing in Hawaii," *The New York Times*, 5 June 1994, http://www.nytimes.com/1994/06/05/us/movement-for-sovereignty-is-growing-in-hawaii.html

27. "Native Hawaiians Seek Redress for U.S. Role in Ousting Queen," *The New York Times*, 11 December 1999, http://www.nytimes.com/1999/12/11/us/native-hawaiians-seek-redress-for-us-role-in-ousting-queen.html

28. Carolyn Said, "Macy's Owner Buying Liberty House," *San Francisco Chronicle*, 22 June 2001, online at http://www.sfgate.com/business/article/Macy-s-owner-buying-Liberty-House-2907331.php

29. Mike Gordon, "The Massie Case," *The Honolulu Advertiser*, 2 July 2006, online at http://the.honoluluadvertiser.com/150/sesq2massiecase

30. Associated Press, "Hawai'i Governor, Police Chief to Review Law Enforcement Response to Palace Takeover," *The Hartford Courant*, 17 August 2008, http://www.courant.com/news/nationworld/nation/wire/sns-ap-palace-takeover,0,307537.story

31. Jennifer Koons, "Supreme Court Backs Hawaii in Land Dispute," *Greenwire* in *The New York Times*, 31 March 2009, http://www.nytimes.com/gwire/2009/03/31/31greenwire-supreme-court-backs-hawaii-in-land-dispute-10366.html

32. "Climate Change Threatens Endangered Honeycreeper Birds of Hawai'i," *Science Daily*, 27 May 2009, online at http://www.sciencedaily.com/releases/2009/05/090526140840.htm

33. "In Hawai'i, Birds' Friday Night Flights Turn Out the Lights on Prep Games," *Associated Press* in *The New York Times*, 24

October 2010, page SP10, online at
http://www.nytimes.com/2010/10/24/sports/24birds.html?hpw

34. Jesse McKinley, "As the Mainland Shivers, Hawai'i Basks in Tourism's Glow," *The New York Times*, 16 February 2011, online at
http://www.nytimes.com/2011/02/17/us/17hawaii.html?_r=1&hp

35. Adam Nagourney, "For Honolulu's Homeless, an Eviction Notice, *The New York Times*, 14 March 2011, page A22, online at
http://www.nytimes.com/2011/03/15/us/15homeless.html?_r=1&hpw

36. Gustave Axelson, "The U.S. Issue: An Eden for Rare Birds in Hawai'i," *The New York Times*, 15 May 2011, page TR5, online at
http://travel.nytimes.com/2011/05/15/travel/treks-through-kauai-exotic-and-bittersweet.html?ref=travel&pagewanted=all

37. Lawrence Downes, "My Kailua," *The New York Times*, 4 September 2011, page TR4, online at
http://travel.nytimes.com/2011/09/04/travel/return-to-kailua-hawaii.html?pagewanted=all

38. David Venditta, "Pearl Harbor Radar Men are Reunited at Allentown," *The Morning Call*, 3 December 2011, online at
http://articles.mcall.com/2011-12-03/news/mc-pearl-harbor-radar-vets-reunited-20111203_1_radar-unit-pearl-harbor-joseph-lockard

39. Associated Press, "Hawai'i lawmaker: Oracle CEO Ellison plans no major upheaval on Lana'i after big land buy," *The Washington Post*, 23 June 2012, online at
http://www.washingtonpost.com/national/biographer-flashy-oracle-founder-likely-to-go-epic-with-next-big-buy-_-a-hawaiian-island/2012/06/21/gJQAfVkNtV_story.html

40. Reuters, "Oracle CEO Ellison Buys Hawai'i's Lana'i Island – No Price Revealed But Pegged at Over $500 Million," *The Chicago Tribune*, 23 June 2012, online at
http://articles.chicagotribune.com/2012-06-21/business/chi-oracle-ceo-larry-ellison-buys-hawaiis-lanai-island-20120621_1_pineapple-fields-hawaii-s-lanai-sixth-largest-island

Bibliography

Legal and Legislative History

41. Kamehameha III and His Government. LAWS OF HIS MAJESTY KAMEHAMEHA III, KING OF THE HAWAI'IAN ISLANDS, PASSED BY THE NOBLES AND REPRESENTATIVES AT THEIR SESSION, 1853. Honolulu, Hawaii: Printed by Order of the Government. 1856.

42. Thomas H. Ball. AGAINST THE ANNEXATION OF HAWAI'I: SPEECH OF THE HON. THOS. H. BALL OF TEXAS, IN THE HOUSE OF REPRESENTATIVES. Wednesday, June 15th, 1898.

43. E.A. Mott-Smith, Secretary of Hawai'i. ELECTION LAWS OF HAWAI'I. Honolulu, Territory of Hawaii: Hawaiian Gazette, Co., Ltd. July 15th, 1910.

44. LAWS OF THE REPUBLIC OF HAWAI'I, PASSED BY THE LEGISLATIVE ASSEMBLY, SPECIAL SESSION. Honolulu, Territory of Hawai'i: Robert Grieve, Steam Book and Job Printer. 1895.

45. Henry E. Chambers. CONSTITUTIONAL HISTORY OF HAWAI'I. Herbert B. Adams, Editor. Baltimore, Maryland: The Johns Hopkins Press. 1896.

46. Kalakaua Rex and Government. LAWS OF THE HAWAI'IAN ISLANDS RELATING TO AGRICULTURE AND FORESTRY. Honolulu, Hawai'i: The Hawai'ian Gazette Company. 1898.

47. Chief Justices Alexander George Morison Robertson and James Leslie Coke, and Associate Justices Ralph Petty Quarles, James Leslie Coke, Samuel Barnet Kemp, and William Seabrook Edings. HAWAI'I REPORTS, VOLUME 24: CASES DECIDED IN THE SUPREME COURT OF THE TERRITORY OF HAWAI'I – AUGUST 1, 1917 TO JUNE 23, 1919. Honolulu, Territory of Hawai'i: Honolulu Star-Bulletin, Ltd. 1919.

48. Hawai'ian People [Hawai'ian Language Edition]. UNIVERSAL DECLARATION OF HUMAN RIGHTS. Honolulu, Hawai'i: Hawai'i Institute for Human Rights. 1948.

Travelogues

49. Isabella Bird. THE HAWAI'IAN ARCHIPELAGO: SIX MONTHS AMONG THE PALM GROVES, CORAL REEFS, VOLCANOES OF THE SANDWICH ISLANDS. Illustrated. Barnes & Noble E-Book: Girlebooks. 1875.

50. Brian Lawrenson. HAWAI'I ALOHA. *U.S.A. Canada Series.* Smashwords Edition. 2011.

Travel Guides

51. Jeannette Foster. HAWAI'I DAY BY DAY. Frommer's 1ST Edition. Hoboken, New Jersey: Wiley's Publishing, Inc. 2010.

52. Rita Ariyoshi. HAWAI'I. Washington, D.C.: National Geographic Traveler. 2009.

53. United States Army Service Forces, Special Service Division. POCKET GUIDE TO HAWAI'I. August 7, 1945.

Hawaiian Language Guides

54. Kahikahealani Wight, Illustrated by Robin Yoko Racoma. ILLUSTRATED HAWAI'IAN DICTIONARY – POCKET EDITION. 3rd Printing. Honolulu, Hawai'i: Bess Press. 2009.

55. BOOK FOR TRAVELERS. Filiquarian Publishing Language Books. Hawai'i: Barnes & Noble Hawai'ian Phrase E-Book. 2011.

Archaeology

56. Van James. ANCIENT SITES OF HAWAI'I: ARCHAEOLOGICAL PLACES OF INTEREST ON THE BIG ISLAND. 5th Edition. Honolulu, Hawai'i: Mutual Publishing. 2005.

Nature Guides and Natural Histories

57. William Tufts Brigham. MEMOIRS OF THE BERNICE PAUAHI BISHOP MUSEUM OF POLYNESIAN HISTORY AND ETHNOLOGY, VOLUME II: THE VOLCANOES OF KILAUEA AND MAUNA LOA ON

Bibliography

THE ISLAND OF HAWAI'I, THEIR VARIOUSLY RECORDED HISTORY TO THE PRESENT TIME. Honolulu, Hawai'i: Bernice Pauahi Bishop Museum Press. 1906-1909.

58. Leland Miyano and Douglas Peebles [Photographs]. A POCKET GUIDE TO HAWAI'I'S FLOWERS. Honolulu, Hawai'i: Mutual Publishing. 1997.

59. Clayton and Michele Oslund. HAWAIIAN GARDENS ARE TO GO TO: A TREASURY OF TROPICAL PLANTS AND GARDENS. Duluth, Minnesota: Plant Pics. 1998.

60. H. Douglas Pratt [Text]. Jack Jeffrey and H. Douglas Pratt [Photographs]. A POCKET GUIDE TO HAWAI'I'S BIRDS. Honolulu, Hawai'i: Mutual Publishing. 2002.

61. H. Douglas Pratt [Text and Photographs]. A POCKET GUIDE TO HAWAI'I'S TREES AND SHRUBS. Honolulu, Hawai'i: Mutual Publishing. 2004.

62. Hawai'i Audubon Society. HAWAI'I'S BIRDS. Honolulu, Hawai'i: Island Heritage Publishing. 2005.

News Videos

63. Avi Lewis. INSIDE USA – THE OTHER HAWAI'I – SEPT 26 – PART 1. *AlJazeeraEnglish* – YouTube Video. September 26, 2008. Online at http://www.youtube.com/watch?v=gIq8x9vnLf4&feature=relmfu

64. Avi Lewis. INSIDE USA – THE OTHER HAWAI'I – SEPT 26 – PART 2. *AlJazeeraEnglish* – YouTube Video. September 26, 2008. Online at http://www.youtube.com/watch?v=1QqOJGSKGWQ&feature=relmfu

Movies and Documentaries

65. Vivian Ducat. HAWAI'I'S LAST QUEEN: THE EMBATTLED REIGN OF QUEEN LILI'UOKALANI. Narrated by David McCullough II and Anna Deveare Smith. PBS: American Experience. 1997.

66. Marc Forby. PRINCESS KAʻIULANI. Starring Q'orianka Kilcher, Barry Pepper, and Will Patton. Produced by Matador Pictures, Island Film Group, and Trailblazer Films. 2009.

67. Mick Kalber. VOLCANOSCAPES V: HAWAIʻI VOLCANOES NATIONAL PARK – AN HISTORICAL PERSPECTIVE. Narrated by Dunbar Wakayama. Produced and edited by G.B. Hajim and Mick Kalber. Hilo, Hawaiʻi: Tropical Visions, Inc. 1996.

68. Atlantis Submarines Hawaiʻi. ATLANTIS SUBMARINES: WAIKIKI – MAUI – KONA. EXPERIENCE OUR HAWAIʻI. Atlantis Submarines, YNR Marketing. 2010.

69. Blue Hawaiʻian Helicopters. VISIONS OF HAWAIʻI: BIG ISLAND – MAUʻI – MOLOKAʻI – LANAʻI – KAUAʻI – OʻAHU. Featuring the music of Kealiʻi Reichel and Amy Hanaialiʻi. Narrated by Pulama Collier. Produced and directed by David J. Chevalier. 2012.

Glossary of Hawaiian Words

Hawaiian was solely an oral language for approximately a millennia and a half, from 300 C.E., when they first arrived at the eight islands in their long na wa'a (canoes) to 1800 C.E. The Hawaiian people kept records of their cultural history, their individual histories, and their way of life by memorizing it all and writing beautiful lyrics to describe it, singing it at births, significant life events, deaths, and whatever else. They have had a long tradition of creating unique songs that are specifically for one person. Such a song is sung when someone is born, and again when they die. Hawaiians measured time in generations, and referred to nights, not days.

Then, in the early 19th century, some Christian missionaries from the United States – New England – took it upon themselves to travel to Hawai'i and teach their religion and culture to the people there. The fact that the Hawaiians were perfectly happy and had a rich and complex culture of their own was utterly irrelevant to the newcomers.

The New Englanders were Calvinists who, like many Christian Caucasians before them, were absolutely convinced that their way of life was better than that of the people whose country they were visiting. Determined to teach the Hawaiians Christianity, along with their own attitude that work would bring one closer to divinity and that sex for any reason other than procreation was a bad thing, they set to work.

The first thing that the missionaries realized they would have to do was to learn the Hawaiian language. Without doing that, they would not be able to communicate any of their own allegedly better ideas about life to the people they sought to indoctrinate. This meant writing down what they heard and learned phonetically using the letter system that they were used to.

The result of this is that when Hawaiians began to write their language, they were using a European-based character system.

The Hawaiian language is more about vowels than about consonants.

There are 5 vowels, just as there are in English, French, and many languages of European origin:

A, E, I, O, U

Hawaiʻi – Stolen Paradise

They are pronounced the same way that French vowels are pronounced:

A, as when a doctor asks a patient to open her/his mouth and say "aah" – like "watch".

E, as in the word "cake".

I, as in "feet".

O, as in "boat".

U, as in "boot".

There are 8 consonants, but one of them is not a letter:

H, K, L, M, N, P, W, and the *okina*.

The okina looks like an upside down apostrophe, and is a glottal stop in word pronunciation.

It looks like this: ʻ

There is also something called a *kahako*.

The kahako is a horizontal line that goes over vowels – over the A and the U.

Any letter with a kahako over it gets a double-length pronunciation.

Unfortunately, many electronic readers don't support software that includes this symbol, and this book was written for electronic media first, so it won't appear here. It is better to have the correct letter be visible to the reader than to see only a portrait-oriented, rectangular box where a letter with a kahako should be. At least with the letter showing, the reader won't be as confused or forced to guess whether the box represents an "a" or a "u" with a kahako.

Here is a list of words that I encountered both as I studied for my trip to Hawaiʻi and as I traveled in the country/state:

aliʻi = aristocrat, chiefly caste.

Glossary

ali'i nui = high chief or king.

Aloha = Hello, Good-bye, may the breath of Heaven be with you.

hale = house.

haole = foreigner. This can often mean white person, but a white person who lives in Hawai'i is not a haole. The word is pronounced "how-lay".

hoku = star.

honu = turtle.

kahili = feather standard carried in pairs by ali'i attendants, and also waved over them as fans.

kahuna = learned advisor, guru. When combined with another word, it is more specific, denoting the discipline that the advisor has studied and practiced, such as priest, doctor, politician, professor in whatever field, etc.

kanaka = native Hawai'ian person.

kane = man.

kapu = taboo, forbidden, sanctified.

kauhale = royal compound of houses and related buildings.

kuhina nui = queen regent.

lahui = people.

lanai = veranda, balcony.

lu'au = feast.

mahalo = thank you.

mo'i = king or queen; first used by Kamehameha III.

na = peaceful. With a kahako over the vowel, it is plural for "the".

Hawai'i – Stolen Paradise

ohana = family.

ono = delicious.

pono = kosher, okay.

wahine = woman.

And here are some place names and a sentence:

Honolulu = Sheltered Bay.

Pu'uloa = Pearl Harbor.

Ke amau mana nui. = Be endowed with more power, spiritual strength, and authority.

About the Author

Stephanie C. Fox, J.D. is a historian, writer, and editor. She is a graduate of William Smith College and the University of Connecticut School of Law. She lives in Connecticut.

She runs an editing and publishing service called *QueenBeeEdit*, found at www.queenbeeedit.com, which caters to politicians, scientists, and others. Her imprint is *QueenBeeBooks*.

Ms. Fox has written several books on a variety of topics, including the effects of human overpopulation on the environment, Asperger's, cats, and travel to Kuwait.

Her areas of interest include – but are not limited to – history, biographies, women's studies, science fiction, human overpopulation, ecosystems collapse, law, international relations, Asperger's, and cats.

www.ingramcontent.com/pod-product-compliance
Lightning Source LLC
Chambersburg PA
CBHW070629300426
44113CB00010B/1715